BEYOND MY STORY . . .
I AM

Opening Doors to Awareness:
a Soulful Journey for the Feminine Spirit

C. Hawks

BALBOA.
PRESS

A DIVISION OF HAY HOUSE

Balboa Press books may be ordered through booksellers or by contacting:

Balboa Press
A Division of Hay House
1663 Liberty Drive
Bloomington, IN 47403
www.balboapress.com
1 (877) 407-4847

Print information available on the last page.

ISBN: 978-1-9822-2328-1 (sc)
ISBN: 978-1-9822-2330-4 (hc)
ISBN: 978-1-9822-2329-8 (e)

Library of Congress Control Number: 2019902685

Balboa Press rev. date: 05/20/2019

With Deep Appreciation and Gratitude

I want to express my gratitude to the three greatest teachers and mentors that could have possibly graced my path. Without the three of you, your own conscious evolution, and blazing of trails, my life would look very different. I sought teachers at a young age and I first found you, Dr. Wayne Dyer. The year was 1976, and I was eighteen years old. Wayne Dyer you rocked my world and I spent the next forty-two years reading every book your wrote, listening to your CD programs, attending your seminars that were within reach, and watching your PBS Specials. You have been an extraordinary guide, teacher, and mentor. Then nineteen years later in 1995, you led me to the writings and teachings of Dr. Deepak Chopra and Dr. David Simon.

Deepak and David, you have taught me not only the most profound healing practices, but you have also provided the experience of ultimate well-being through your healing programs consisting of nourishing Ayurvedic meals, panchakarma treatments, and meditation. You offered the experience of wellness at a soul level, and set me on a path to Enlightenment. Your books, seminars, CD's, and DVD programs continue to guide my life.

Without the three of you I wouldn't have had a clue how to begin this inquisitive healing journey.

A million thank-you's!

Dedication

To my children –

You are my constant inspiration for
choosing a path to Enlightenment.

Thank you for choosing me to play the role of
mother and friend in this incarnation.

Contents

Introduction

ave you ever wanted to run away? Have you wanted to step out of your life for a day, a week, a month, forever? Have you wanted to hop on an international flight and go to an enchanting faraway land and hang out in little villages steeped in history and not know a soul? Have you ached for consecutive days, weeks, and months with no mail to open; nothing to handle today? Have you yearned for moments in time where nobody can ask anything of you? Where nobody even knows exactly where you are just for a spell. Have you ever reached a point of *enough*! The feeling that you've had *enough* of these overwhelming, stress filled days. You know, the days where you open your eyes in the morning and the very act of opening your eye lids was about as much energy as you had to exert for the entire day. Me too!

So I did it! I woke up one morning about five weeks ago and I said *"Enough, I'm out."* I am going to get on an airplane, step out of my life as I know it, and go find not only me, but also the life that is out there waiting for me to show up and live it. On June 7, I boarded an international flight from Seattle Tacoma International Airport to London Heathrow International Airport. And my mantra in those weeks leading up to June 7 was "Please God do not let me die of a stroke or a heart attack from all of this damn stress before I get on the *f**king plane*." As the *Universe* would have it, I did not die. I got on the plane. I was too tired to feel anxious about my decision and about seven hours into the overnight flight, for the first time in a long time, I felt the faint whispers of an old familiar smile flicker deep inside of me. I used to have a lot of those deep inside of me smiles. I used to have moments and months and years where I would think if I died tomorrow I've sure had a great time. That flicker of a smile was my first memory of those deep soul smiles in a long, long time.

I'm not quite sure when it was that life became so heavy, so much to carry, so much stress and exhaustion. When did my thoughts become permeated with these never ending questions: "What's happening to me? Where did I go? Where is my 'happy' place? Where is my energy? Why all of these stressful thoughts? Where am I? Who am I? Why am I? Have I lost sight of me? When? Why do I fill with tears so easily? What the hell has happened to me?"

I think that we all must reach moments in our lives where there is so much overwhelm. When situations, people, events, and life just pile up and weigh heavy on our spirits. Or better said, when we put too much of our attention on the situations, people, and life events that show up. I find myself in new territory. It seems I have been managing and juggling lots and lots and lots throughout my adult life; what has felt like an endless amount of challenges. But I was also always able to maintain a happiness and joy factor. My default reaction to almost any situation that life has thrown my way has been to greet it with laughter or at least know that at some moment I would laugh about it. I've always had this uncanny ability to roll with the challenging times that present themselves. Why am I struggling now? I know how to live happy and well. I have life practices in place that ensure my level of vibrancy, humor, and strength. So what the heck is going on?

This is my fifty-ninth summer. I have been studying with the greats like Wayne Dyer, Deepak Chopra, David Simon, and others for four decades. I have metabolized a level of awareness that helps me to maneuver through life with at least some level of grace. I have been practicing meditation since 1995 and teaching the practice since 1996. And I have been supporting others on their journeys – always. So what's my story? How have I been defining myself, my life, and ultimately my way of being in the world? What needs to be examined, rethought, and redefined?

Over the years I have become crucially aware of the immense power that our stories hold. Our stories, the things we focus on and share with others; and the ways we define ourselves and our lives. Like everything, our stories vibrate to a frequency. Every thought we have contains within it a frequency. Examples of the lower frequencies are thoughts and feelings of shame, guilt, judgment, sadness, anger, frustration, worry, fear, and intolerance. Examples of higher frequencies are thoughts and feelings of peace, joy, love, grace, laughter, happiness, and fulfillment. When did my story change? Why did my story change? Why am I feeling the exhaustion and the sadness that I'm feeling? What the hell is my story? And if I am the author of my story, where the hell did I get so off track?

I would love to peg my whole de-transformation on the election of Donald Trump as our President. Gosh, even saying those words brings a particular sadness. It is disparaging isn't it? To be brutally honest, there is actually truth value in being impacted by the election of Trump. There are so many of us in the United States and in the world that have been experiencing differing levels of sadness and anger that a person so driven by ego and all things unfortunate could have possibly been elected to lead one of the greatest nations in the world. In trying to make sense of things after the election, I remember sitting one evening and Googling "What do our spiritual teachers think about this presidential election?"

I found an interview conducted by CNN with Deepak Chopra sharing his thoughts about Donald Trump. The interview took place about five months before the election. Deepak shared that it had been a difficult decision for him to be public about his insights and feelings about Donald Trump but that ultimately he thought it would be a necessary and positive thing for all of us to hear. I am very grateful that Deepak decided to share because it has helped me. He talked about how, in his opinion, Donald Trump represents a darkness that exists in all of us; that he is driven by ego, and that he has the emotional intelligence of a three year old. The most important thing that I think Deepak shared is that we can only meet the darkness with light. It is our responsibility to each find the path through our own darkness to the light within and to embody that light. It has never been so straight forwardly apparent that each of us has the responsibility to consciously evolve. We have been given the perfect role model in Donald Trump as someone who has not elected to pursue this higher frequency of thought and Being. Donald Trump's actions and behaviors epitomize the darkest shadow that exists as a possibility within each of us.

All of that aside, I think that the political climate in the United States certainly contributed to my loss of sense of happiness but more than anything else it was my story, the story I was living out loud that had been dropping me to my knees.

So I am off and away to examine my story, to learn from my story, and to move beyond my story. That is assuming of course, that I have the courage to be brutally honest with myself and a tenacious spirit to see me through. Right now, I'm just exhausted and barely holding together.

We are travelers on a journey to the heart of life. In our own way and in our own time, each of us is on a path that leads from constriction to expansion, from limitation to infinite possibilities, from fear to love, and from separation to unity.

David Simon
Deepak Chopra

Chapter One

I Didn't Die – I Got on the Plane

My flight departed at 11:43 p.m. It was a direct flight from SeaTac Airport to London Heathrow. A nine-and-a-half-hour flight and an eight-hour time change. I didn't sleep a wink. I was way too tired to sleep. I watched four in-flight movies, *kind of sort of.* But mostly I gazed out the window and breathed small breaths of relief that I was actually on the plane and flying to a faraway land. A small tender smile was finding its way to my lips. I didn't care how long the flight took or even if we ever landed. I was marveling at the fact that I had actually done it. I got on the damn plane and I had ninety-two days before I would be on my return flight home. Ninety-two days. What would that feel like? I have traveled to Europe many times in my life but never like this and never for this length of time. I suspected that I would get homesick, miss the people I love, and miss my home and my own bed. I also knew that I had to get me right before returning home. For me, this was a "Put on your oxygen mask first" trip. I had never been this out of sorts. I had never reached a point of screaming "Uncle!" to the *Universe* and declaring that I had had *enough*! I knew that I needed to examine the story I was living and rewrite that sucker before it killed me. Yes, that's exactly what I mean, before my own story killed me. I also have enough wisdom to know that long before any rewrite could take place, I had to trudge through the process of a brutally honest look at myself, my thoughts, and the consciousness that has shaped those thoughts. This journey is about the trudging.

When I booked my trip, just weeks before I left, I knew there had to be three major components to it. I desperately needed deep and profound rest and healing. Then I needed a waking-up period to find myself and my energy again. The last component would be to get strong mentally, physically, spiritually, and emotionally. I booked the front twenty-one days of my trip and the last twenty-eight days and was not sure how the middle part would unfold. I chose to fly in and out of Heathrow because I have really dear friends I wanted to spend a few days with on the front and back ends of my journey.

On June 8, I landed safe and sound at Heathrow and stood in the "Non EU Citizen Line" for well over an hour to clear customs. After officials determined that I was a threat only to myself and not a threat to international security, I was cleared to exit through the double doors that stated "Nothing to Declare." The only thing I could possibly think to declare would have been my insanity. I actually laughed a little inside as I was waiting in the long customs line and thinking about my response to their typical question "Purpose of your trip?" My response would be "I'm running away, sir. I've had enough. I said 'Uncle!' to the *Universe*, got on a plane, and here I am. As much as I can tell, life has dealt me a huge amount of shit to deal with these past several years, and I believe it is due to the fact that I was an axe murderer in a previous life. And I must have enjoyed it given the massive load of crap that has come my way of late." I think I actually giggled out loud. When I reached the front of the line, I chose only to say, "Pleasure is the purpose of my trip." Because Lord knows there has been a huge absence of that lately.

I was filling with excitement as I exited that door. One of the *"peeps"* who I have embraced as a member of my family would be waiting for me right outside that door. It had been seven years since I'd seen James. *I think.* There was no question if I would recognize him or not. It is hard to miss a six-foot, seven-inch handsome Aussie with a big, shit-eating grin on his face. *Oh my God, there he is! I see him! I'm really here. I really did it! And I am still standing.* James's hugs always feel like his arms are wrapped around me three times. Oh my God, it is so good to see him. I feel so warm and safe with James. He is a truly lovely soul. His humor is right up my alley, and while it's definitely not for the meek, I adore him. My lovely daughter brought James to our family for inspection in 2002, after she met him while studying abroad in Australia. They dated for five years while traveling back and forth to each other's country. The distance took its toll on their relationship, but James has remained "family" in our hearts and forever will be. It was Thursday, midday, and I would stay with James and his lady in their London flat for four days before heading out on my own for part one, deep rest and healing.

I thought that James would be working all day on Friday, but to my surprise, he had taken Thursday afternoon and Friday off and had made plans to entertain me. And that he did. I felt that all I had in me was the energy to collapse, but I was also deeply touched by his kindness. He had plans for Friday, Saturday, and Sunday and never shared a word of the details with me. Thank goodness we were in London where people are so much more accepting of one another. Not having a clue where we were going, I was clad in my extremely loved Lululemon exercise wear. Who knew that I would be shopping at the famous Liberty store or taking in a local play?

We walked and walked and walked around outlying neighborhoods of London and all the way to Greenwich Village, the Greenwich Mean Time Observatory, and into London proper.

We did not do the normal touristy things that most people do in London. During previous trips, I had visited the iconic Big Ben and Westminster Abbey and the torture chambers in the Tower of London. I had taken a ride on the London Eye and visited Buckingham Palace, as well as many of the fabulous London art galleries. Instead, James and I walked through neighborhoods that were off the beaten path, shopped at the local markets, enjoyed Guinness at the corner pubs, and took in London as it is lived by the local people.

We did stop to enjoy art at the Tate Modern Gallery, where one of my favorite trip photos was taken of me in front of a larger-than-life-size photo of a man's hairy bum and genitals. In the photo, I am pointing to the center of the image. I should have listened to James; he told me to smell my finger for the photo. That would have been much more fun, but there were passersby and I was a tad bit shy.

Our evenings were filled with eating amazing foods from small, neighborhood vendors. We ate African, Afghanistan, Jamaican, and home-cooked meals, all of which were a delight to the senses; delicious food with the mouthwatering essence of other cultures.

There were so many highlights during my time with James. I did fall asleep a couple of times during our adventures because I was in such a state of mental, emotional, and physical exhaustion. However, I did not fall asleep during my favorite event.

On Saturday around midday, James said "Okay, Azul we've got to get going and catch a bus." James had nicknamed me "Azul" years ago when we first met because that is what some Aussies call redheads in Australia. Or at least that's the story James told me. Again, I had not a clue where we were heading. We hopped off the bus in the center of London, and James with his long-legged stride had me running after him. After several blocks of thinking *"Holy shit I think my legs are going to fall off!"* we walked up a side street with a long line of people waiting outside an old British theater. James bypassed the line, went inside, and asked for two tickets in his name, and then we raced into the theater. I had no idea that the play we were about to see was *The Book of Mormon.* It turned out to be the best and funniest play I have ever seen in my life. Part of the joy of the experience was seeing it with James, who has the most absurd, magical sense of humor. And another part is that the play is just hysterical. I ached from laughter during the play, and my cheeks ached for hours afterward. It was so good for my soul to laugh like that. I think my body almost went into convulsions after not having experienced that level of laughter for so long.

On Sunday, James again surprised me with a drive to Bath in southwest England, where we explored the ancient Roman Baths that had been used for public bathing as early as the first-century AD. Bath is a charming eighteenth-century village with Georgian architecture. In the morning, we ate delicious cream-filled pastries in a quaint little bakery with views to the river. By midday, we were feasting on fish and chips in a proper British pub in the main square. On the way home, we stopped at Stonehenge, the prehistoric monument dating back as far as 3000 BC. It was absolutely mesmerizing. In all of my trips to England and Wales over the years, I had never been to either place.

On Monday, James returned to work, and I slept for half of the day. During the evening I packed for my early morning flight on June 13. As I packed I felt full of wonder about the place I had chosen for the deep rest and healing that I so longed for. On the one hand, I hoped it would be a top notch healing program. And on the other hand, I just cared that there would be a comfortable bed and a room filled with quiet to bring ease to the ache that permeated my Being.

James had been the most gracious host, and we promised to try to see each other in three months when I would be back in London for my final days of this sojourn. On Tuesday morning at 4:30 a.m., James had set his alarm so he could walk with me down the street to the hired car which would take me to Heathrow for my flight to Stuttgart, Germany. From Stuttgart I would travel another ninety-eight kilometers to a little village, Schwabisch Hall, where I would stay for twenty-one days at a place called the Shakti Center.

This is the front end of the trip that I had pre-booked for the deep and profound healing and rest that I so desperately needed. The Shakti Center offered Ayurvedic meals and panchakarma treatments. I will say a little bit about these terms; however, if these terms are not familiar to you, I encourage you to read Deepak Chopra's book *Perfect Health* to learn more about each. The literal translation of Ayurveda is "Science of Life," and is a 5,000 year old healing system from the Vedic tradition of India. Panchakarma consists of very specific healing massage treatments that are nourishing, detoxing, rejuvenating, and euphoric. Dr. Deepak Chopra and Dr. David Simon have worked diligently for decades to marry these Eastern philosophies of health and well-being with Western Medicine. In his book, *Free to Love Free to Heal,* Dr. Simon shares that "Ayurveda offers a valuable approach to emotional and physical health – a holistic perspective that recognizes that the two are, in fact, inseparable."

I first discovered Deepak Chopra in 1995, after I had ruptured a disk in my lower back. I was thirty-seven years old and absolutely debilitated by sciatic pain. I was crawling on my hands and knees around my home and my daughter had to help me dress in the mornings. If any of you have experienced sciatic pain, you know exactly what I am talking about. I was terrified. I was fearful that I would be disabled for the rest of my life. I did not want to have surgery. I was trying to tolerate the pain, while continuing to play the role of single mom, with a nine-year-old son and a sixteen-year-old daughter. I was scared skinny. During those months of excruciating pain, people often asked how I hurt my back. My response was "From carrying the weight of the world on my shoulders." My comment was typically met with suspicion and remarks like "No really, how did you injure your back?" Today, my answer remains, "From carrying the weight of the world on my shoulders." But now I would add, "My thinking made it so."

It was mid-afternoon one day during those long and difficult months, that I laid on my stomach on my family room floor in an attempt to alleviate the pain, and turned on the television;

something that I would never do in the normal course of a weekday. There, on the screen, was Deepak talking about back health. He captivated my interest and after the show was over, I set out to find Dr. Deepak Chopra. I did end up electing to have back surgery in January 1995, and then with post-surgery sutures still in place, I traveled to Del Mar, California and entered Drs. Chopra and Simon's residential health and wellness program. That healing week, and all of the magical experiences, was absolutely transformative. There were twelve of us in that group. We ate Ayurvedic meals every day. We received panchakarma treatments every day. We learned to meditate and practiced Thai Chi. We had classes with Deepak and David every day. Several members of our small group had, prior to that program, been given a terminal diagnosis and had tried everything Western medicine had to offer. They were present to heal and to find peace. It was one of the most extraordinary and memorable weeks of my life, and dear friendships were born.

When I was booking the front end of my sojourn, I had googled Europe and Ayurveda, and found the Shakti Center along with many other options. I had no idea how nourishing the Ayurvedic meals would be, how good the panchakarma treatments would be, or how enlightened the practitioners would be. My only reference point was the Chopra Center for Well-Being and everything was first class and first rate at the Chopra Center.

My flight from Heathrow to Stuttgart was incredibly quick. The Shakti Center had arranged a driver for me and informed me that they "Wear red jackets with yellow inscription on the back TRANSFERPRATZ." I spotted a gentleman by that description right away and introduced myself. He did not speak a word of English, and with a very strong German accent, he said "Schvabeesh Hull?" It sounded like it could be my destination so I said, "Yes please," and we were off. I didn't even know how to pronounce the name of the village I was heading to, but I knew it started with the letters schw. I sat in the front passenger seat and the driver and I spoke occasionally and smiled, but neither of us had a clue what the other was saying. I was stunned by the number of *lorries* on the autobahn, leaving from and heading toward, Stuttgart. There were semi-trucks for miles and miles. It was an amazing sight to behold. They must export a lot of product and produce out of Germany. As they should! Nobody builds and produces things as well as the German people, nobody.

During the drive I found myself so relieved to be heading to the Shakti Center for much needed rest. My time in London with James had been magical in all ways, and I had laughed deeply for the first time in a long time, but my level of exhaustion was ever present. I suspected that after I arrived at my destination and settled in, that I might just cry a river of tears for the twenty-one days that I would be there. I needed to detach from my life. I needed to examine the story that I had been living. And I needed to rest. I had never known this level of sheer exhaustion.

As we neared Schwabisch Hall, I felt a growing excitement. I had really done this! I had really stepped out of life as I knew it! I did not have a clue what this experience was going to be like, and I did not know a single soul in the village (or country for that matter) where I would be staying. I think those feelings of such uncertainty scare the heck out of many people. Not me. I loved those feelings of uncertainty and brand, spanking new adventure. So many "wise" friends had suggested that I shouldn't travel alone. Or that I should have put the money in the bank and not spend it so frivolously. Or they tried to instill cautionary levels of doom and gloom. I was not listening to the sage wisdom of the "normals." I was much more terrified not to pursue this adventure. And if I were to die, great! At least it was somewhere new and exciting.

We arrived at the Shakti Center, which is situated right at the entrance to the pedestrian walkway through the village. My relatively short, but freakishly strong, driver hauled my unusually heavy suitcase up three flights of narrow and windy stairs; most definitely an act of kindness worthy of a huge tip. A lovely East Indian woman, Amna, greeted me and gave me a quick tour and orientation. When I first reserved my accommodations here, I received a message from my booking representative that the lead practitioner had called to make sure "She knows that this is not a big resort to stay for twenty-one days. Only three people can stay at a time." I hadn't known that, but it was music to my ears. I wasn't after "resort," I was after profound healing, deep rest, and remembering *Who I Really Am.*

Amna led me up another flight of narrow and windy stairs, and showed me to my room. My room contained two twin beds, which meant that since they can only accommodate three people at a time, there would only be, at most, one other person in residence with me. It was a good sized room with very simple furnishings. On one side, there were two twin beds pushed together with coral-colored comforter covers over light down bedding, and simple wooden side tables on either side of the beds. There was also a tall wardrobe on that side of the room. The other side had a small wooden desk and wooden chair, another wardrobe, a small corner glassed-in-shower with sink and mirror to the left, and a private WC. It was just perfect.

Amna informed me that my first panchakarma treatment would begin at 2:00 p.m. that day. It was now 12:30 p.m. I had no idea that my treatment would begin so soon, and I asked if I could take a quick walk before my 2:00 p.m. appointment. She agreed that I had time for a walk, escorted me back down to the third floor, and showed me the treatment room where I would come for my panchakarma. I left the building, and as I walked the first ten paces and saw the main street of Schwabisch Hall, a big shit-eating grin graced my face. It was magical. A perfect representation of everything that I had seen on the brochure and exactly how I had hoped it would be. This sweet little place is an eleventh-century village, with narrow cobblestone streets, lined with a mixture of small restaurants and patios, shops with gorgeous clothing, high-end kitchen accessories, novelty shops with exquisite pieces of art created by local artisans, children's toys, and a sports store; all intermixed with attached single-family residences. Colorful window-boxes filled with beautiful blossoms adorned the storefronts and lace curtains fluttered in the summer breeze. There were handcrafted, thick, wood shutters hinged in the open position to allow the light of summer to enter, and a tall old stone tutor-topped bell tower at the end of the street. The aroma of fresh-baked bread with a hint of sweetness was in the air. I walked down the cobblestone street to the first restaurant on the right. It had the appearance of an Italian café, and I sat outside on the patio at a little table with a red-and-white-checkered tablecloth and asked the waiter for a glass of red wine. He nodded and brought me a glass of white wine. This was my first hint of the magic of nobody in the village speaking English; which was about to make my trip just that much richer. It was also the beginning of my journey of charades, pantomime, and laughter working together to understand one another.

I had made the decision to race out for a walk more for the glass of wine than for "the walk." I have never been a big drinker in my life, but over the past few years I had added a couple of glasses of red wine to my nightly routine several times a week, and I was fairly certain that this new numbing habit was contributing to the loss of my sense of self and my authentic happiness. It had been my plan to not drink during my twenty-one days of panchakarma and nourishing Ayurvedic meals. So I enjoyed my last two quick glasses of wine and a bite to eat, returned to the Shakti Center, changed into my robe, and met Amna outside of the treatment room; located one floor below my accommodations. She led me into the treatment room and introduced me to the therapist who would give me my panchakarma treatment. Her name was Rathi, a small East Indian woman who spoke no English, and who wore the sweetest smile. The treatment was ninety minutes in length. As I walked into the room, I was overtaken with the memory of wellness that I had achieved after a week at the Chopra Center many, many years ago. The scent of the sesame oil, the music, the look and feel of the room, all sent a rush of wellness through my veins. The next thing I was aware of was waking-up on the treatment table, and for a few minutes having absolutely no idea where I was. I had fallen into such a deep, deep sleep shortly after my treatment began and slept soundly for an hour on the table after the session had ended. And that was just the beginning!

That evening I would also enjoy my first Ayurvedic meal, dinner at 5:00 p.m. The treatment and yoga rooms were located on the second and third floors of the Shakti Center. The first floor had an authentic Indian Restaurant where I thought I would be eating my meals. However, all meals: breakfast, lunch, and dinner every day were served in a private room on the third floor. A perfectly simple room, and in it, an old, wooden, dining table with four chairs, and a matching buffet displaying a selection of delicious healing teas and a hot water kettle. There was also a treatment table in this room and a little sink with a mirror on the opposite wall.

After my panchakarma, I showered and came to dinner at 5:00 p.m. I met a lovely woman who was just finishing her stay and would be leaving first thing in the morning. She had been there for a week healing from the loss of her husband. We visited briefly. She appeared to be a kind woman who spoke very little English, but pain and death can be universally understood if we are being fully present to one another. I was struck now, as I was struck when I first went to the Chopra Center in 1995, by how it seems the majority of people who are drawn to these Eastern healing practices, come after terminal diagnosis or profound loss. After they have tried everything Western medicine has prescribed and recommended. I feel so blessed to have preventative practices in my life, and I feel so blessed to have discovered Ayurveda. My mission is to prevent a diagnosis. And, I think the profound aspects of a preventative practice include: daily meditation, experiencing joy and happiness, expressing gratitude every day, and forgiving everyone of everything as immediately as possible. I might have underestimated my own evolution in undertaking this grand act of healing with just twenty more days of panchakarma, but I remained optimistic. Plus, *who* gets to just step out of life, run away to a little village in Germany, and enjoy twenty-one days of panchakarma and Ayurvedic healing meals? I was fairly certain I could do this and do it well. I was feeling like the most blessed person in the world. Tired but blessed.

For the next twenty days my schedule, with only marginal variations, was this: 7:30 a.m., wake-up and slip into comfortable clothes; 8:00 a.m., my own thirty-minute meditation practice followed by yoga stretches in a quaint yoga room with views out to the garden; 8:45 a.m., breakfast served to me in a private little room; 10:00 a.m., ninety minutes of panchakarma; 12:00 p.m., gorgeous Ayurvedic lunch; all afternoon to rest and another thirty minute meditation; 5:00 p.m., private dinner; and the evening to myself. There were no televisions or radios at the Shakti Center. I enjoyed the inside silence, and I equally enjoyed listening through my open window to the sounds of German speaking adults and children talking and laughing, and the foreignness of it all.

Preparing to let go begins with intentions.

David Simon

Chapter Two

Tip of the Iceberg

During the first week, between lunch and dinner, and during the evenings, I just rested. I was exhausted at a level that I had never known before. In the afternoons, after panchakarma, I would fall into a sleep so deep that I could hear and was aware of my own snoring, and I don't normally snore! In those initial days I was just touching the tip of the iceberg of the rest that I needed. You know how it feels when you have been on your lips tired for too long and then you get a great night's sleep, and you realize just how much more rest you need. Yes? Well, that was my first seven days; profound, delicious, deep rest.

I don't think words can truly describe panchakarma healing treatments, but let me give it a try. For those of you that have not had the experience, I highly recommend that you put it on your bucket list. Of course, depending on the practitioner and the Ayurvedic program that you go to, there may be some variations in how the treatments are performed. Here is a sampling of what my treatments were like at the Shakti Center with Rathi's magical healing energy. I would slip on a white, soft, cotton robe made out of waffle material, and with nothing on underneath, I would walk down one flight of stairs to the treatment room. Each of the treatment rooms had one or two traditional Ayurvedic treatment tables. These ones were imported from India and the legs and bases were made out of beautiful dark wood with ornate designs. Each table had a thin mattress surface, covered with burnt-orange-colored leather. One of the tables had a large brass bowl hanging above the area of the table where you lay your head. The bowl is used for a specific treatment called Shirodhara, where oil is dripped gently on your forehead. I remember the first time I read about Shirodhara before I ever attended The Chopra Center program in 1995. It sounded like a Chinese water-drip torture treatment. I couldn't have been more mistaken. It is bliss and euphoria all wrapped into one big bundle, and at least for me, it was hard to stay conscious. The fragrance of healing oils permeated the entire floor which housed the treatment rooms. Each day a specific combination of oils was designed with precision for my unique healing journey.

Rathi would start by having me sit on a short wooden stool with my robe on. She would begin the ninety-minute regimen by filling her hands with warm healing oils, and gently massage the oils on my hair, scalp, neck and face. She applied just the right amount of pressure and worked in circular motions. Next, she would move to my shoulders, upper back, and arms. I would open the robe and let it drop around my waste. Oh my God, it all felt so blissful; the oil, the deep circular motions, and the brisk friction up and down my arms and between my shoulder blades. I could feel the tension in my upper body start to let go, and my head would bob a bit as the stress was being released. Then it was time to move from sitting on the stool to lying on the table. We always started this portion of the treatment with me lying face down. Rathi would work from the top of my spine all the way to the souls of my feet with her magical healing hands and beautiful energy. Then I would turn over and she would work from the tip of my head all the way to my toes. She used circular motions on my abdomen and around my breasts, and long gliding strokes on the stretches of my body. A unique combination of circular, deep, straight motions with friction all engulfed in the energy of divine healing. I can't begin to express the gratitude I felt every single day for those delicious profoundly healing treatments. Do you want to know what I learned? I *can* make a good decision! *Woot! Woot!*

My first week was also filled with prayers and pleadings to the *Universe* to hear me, to help me, and to show me clarity and provide guidance. I think all of my prayers started with "Dear God, Brahman, Allah, Buddha, Krishna, Jesus, Archangel Michael, Mother Teresa, spirit guides, angels, and transitioned souls, please *help* me remember *Who I Really Am*, help me to heal, and please help my children find their own peace and healing. And Jet, please watch over our son and our daughter and show up as a guide in ways that you couldn't while you were here in your skin encapsulated ego human form. *Please.*" Yes, I called on every evolved Being that I thought I might be able to summon. And I held an *uncompromising* intention to heal!

Jet, my former husband, had died eight months earlier. His was a very quick death; diagnosis, stage IV stomach cancer. He died of neutropenic septic shock on day fourteen of treatment. He named me as his Executor and Trustee and I am still serving in that role as I write today. Jet was a man who I loved deeply, and even though we had divorced over two decades earlier we had remained dear friends and family members. At the time of Jet's death, my life had already been leaning a little sideways for the previous three years. We'll get to those details a little later.

From the moment of Jet's death, my life has been filled with the business of dying. And for so many of you out there who have served as an Executor or Personal Representative for a loved one, you know exactly what I'm talking about. To juggle all of the emotions of loss with the business of dying; the arrangements for the body, the Life Celebration, the obituary, letting friends and family know the details, the lawyers, the banks, the CPA's, the taxes, the creditors, the belongings, and the family. It is endless. I have even lost count of how many idiots there are at the varying levels of bureaucracy who don't really care at all about how they are making the business of dying so much more difficult than need be. Every once in a while I have encountered an *eagle* who is an exceptional and empathic person, but that is very rare indeed. I have found that after many months into this journey, I have a stand up for myself voice that didn't used to be a part of my character. And I like it. The job itself is tiring, emotional, and tough. To also be labeled an "ex-wife" and one of our two children labeled a "step-child" has added a layer of crap to the journey that I haven't enjoyed at all, but it has given me voice. I have also discovered that the vast majority of people assume that I am not suffering a loss because "He was your ex-husband." Really, do most people carry that much resentment and dislike inside of them for their ex-partners? Are we that unforgiving? Do we not yet understand that one of our highest goals should be to forgive everybody of everything as quickly as humanly possible? Those acts of compassion free our souls from attachment and pain. Wayne Dyer taught me a long, long time ago that "It takes much more courage, strength of character, and inner conviction to forgive than it does to hang on to low-energy feelings."

After our divorce, Jet and I had continued our friendship sharing all family birthdays, major holidays, and other events together with our children. We never did "exes" "steps" and "halves" when it came to our children and to our family. The constant encounter of the ignorance of the masses on these very salient issues has definitely made handling the business of dying on Jet's behalf more difficult.

Week one at the Shakti Center was filled with panchakarma, nourishing meals, prayer, and a great deal of rest. I have never been a napper but I can tell you that I did not resist the suggestions that I "Just rest for the afternoons." It was a profound level of rest. I fell into deep, deep sleeps precipitated by deep, deep prayers.

By the beginning of week two, I was feeling immense gratitude for my choice to come on this outstanding little adventure and deep gratitude that I had made such a good choice to come to the Shakti Center in Schwabisch Hall, Germany. I was receiving the first mega dose of nourishment that I so desperately needed; nourishment at every level of my Being. The Ayurvedic meals were also very mindfully designed to complement my healing and detoxification. If you have never tried Ayurvedic meals, add that to your bucket list too. They are typically vegetarian meals and when prepared well contain all of the six tastes (sweet, sour, salty, pungent, bitter, and astringent). Fabulously delicious, nourishing food, and since they contain all six tastes there are no cravings for something more.

During this second week I started to examine the health and well-being of all aspects of my life. I had studied with the greats long enough to have learned that optimal health means health at all levels: emotional well-being, physical well-being, spiritual well-being, relational well-being, and environmental well-being. I would ponder these areas of my life as I walked through the enchanting village, which was so steeped in history and all things foreign. I devoured the smells, the beauty, the people; each facet playing a major role in waking a sleeping part of my soul.

Sudeep, the lead practitioner, and Amna spoke enough English to very thoughtfully design and customize my healing journey. Almost everyone else in the village spoke no English. At first I was a bit stunned by that. I have traveled to various destinations in Europe and it has been very rare not to find many people who could speak English. I anticipated that I would run into no English speakers in Poland, where I would be spending my last twenty-eight days, but I was shocked to find the same here. And I was absolutely over-the-moon delighted. You see, as I started to look at the facets of my life, I was also paying deep and thoughtful attention to my story that feeds each of these facets. Part of the beauty of no English speakers was that I could not continue to unconsciously share any aspects of my story. Nor could I understand their stories. It was all extremely magical. No drama shared. No drama received. This is not to say that I didn't engage with people. I engaged with people every time I went for a walk in the village. However, the encounters were more like pantomime and charades, and the occasional exchange of a German word, that I had rolled around in my mouth long enough to have it come out sounding like something remotely detectable as language. Heck, it took me an entire three days just to pronounce Schwabisch Hall correctly!

Prior to departing for my trip, I actually thought that once I arrived in Germany for twenty-one days of Ayurvedic healing, I would just melt into a pool of tears and let everything, whatever the hell it was, out. But instead I found myself beaming from ear to ear at just being there. From day one, I beamed at being present there. I don't know about you, but I adore being steeped in history. I love, love, love Europe! Not to deny that I had some serious healing and self-awareness (*awarefulness*) journeying to do, but I was also experiencing the sweetness of feeling "Look at you girl! Look at where you are right now! You've made an outstanding choice my dear. *Wahoo!*" Love that voice! How had I let that voice get buried? And buried by what? What the heck had I been putting out into the *Universe*? My entire focus on this sojourn was to become deeply aware. I like defining that as achieving *awarefulness* – a state of being extremely self-aware, which at least for me is the path to manifesting health, wholeness, and enlightenment.

Before I jump into looking at the various thoughts that inform and guide the facets of my life, I want to pause and express my deep, deep gratitude to the angels, guides, Gods, shamans, and spirits that held me upright long enough to guide my decision making to get on that damn plane and go to a faraway land. Thank you. Thank you. Thank you.

You must become the producer, and the actor
in the unfolding story of your life.

Wayne Dyer

Chapter Three

And So the Story Goes

W
here to begin? Recognizing that all aspects of my life are interdependent and enveloped in the chaos that I have felt, I'll start with an examination of the environmental facets of my life. As I explore each of these areas, you will begin to understand my earlier comments about my life being a bit sideways for the past several years. And dear Reader, do not think for a single minute that you are off the hook. Yes, I am embarking on this journey to *awarefulness* for me. And it is my hope that in doing so, that I may also serve as a guide for you to begin your own journey to *awarefulness,* by encouraging you to examine your own story and to deepen your own questioning about *who you are* and *why you are.*

Environmental factors include my home and living situation, the larger geographical area, and the shared or lack of shared experiences. I think that tracing back a bit, will provide you with a broad context to juxtapose against your own environmental health and well-being. I was born a small, black boy in Red Deer, Alberta, Canada. Not really, I'm just messing with you. I was born a small, redheaded, white girl in Red Deer, Alberta, Canada and was raised in Calgary for eight years until my mom's soon to be second husband (and my new father) was transferred to the United States and my mom, siblings, and I followed within a year. I spent my growing up years moving back and forth between Idaho and Washington. Life happened, and lots of it. In 1983 I married my husband, Jet, and in 1984 we moved to Seattle, Washington with our five-year-old daughter. I adore the beauty of the Pacific Northwest. I love the ocean, the mountains, the islands, the rain forest, the lakes and rivers, and breathing the sweet ocean air. The natural beauty is breathtaking. I spend a lot of time in nature; walking, boating, and going barefoot whenever I can. So the natural environment part of my life and my life story has been a strong point since moving to the Pacific Northwest.

I have been blessed to live in some extremely incredible homes in the greater Seattle area. We raised our children in what used to be the "country," and then it exploded with newcomers and became the "burbs" as some of the mega businesses like Microsoft, Starbucks, and Amazon boomed. In 2005, I moved to one of Seattle's most historic and coveted neighborhoods, which I had been introduced to through colleagues in 1985. It took me a while to get there, but when I did living in this neighborhood turned out to be everything that I imagined it would be, and more. I enjoyed life in this magical neighborhood until I was swept off my feet by a man, of course.

This man galloped into my life on a handsome black steed. He had presented himself to be a kind, honest, funny, attractive, loving, available, wealthy, and devoted man. And after eighteen months of his hot pursuit, I took the leap and left my life in Seattle. As fate would have it, my birth father also lived in the same larger geographical area that I was considering relocating to. I wanted a chance to get to know my father, who I had only seen maybe four times since I was thirteen years old. So off I went. I packed up my life, sold many of my cherished belongings, and promised my grown children that I would be back as often as possible to see them. And that ultimately, and within a year, I would have a presence in Seattle again. It was an incredibly scary decision to leave the environment that I adored so much and that soothed my soul, but this man promised that he would fly me home every month.

When I get to the discussion on relationships, I'll share more of the details on how the relationship with the man on the handsome steed turned out. Right now, suffice it to say that within eighteen months I was back in Seattle and spent six months couch surfing while I tried to piece my life back together.

Once back home, I was looking for a small condo to buy in my old neighborhood. It was the beginning of 2015 and the market had rebounded from the recession, and as is characteristic of Seattle, it was very strong and expensive housing market. So I extended my search to include our neighboring island communities, one of which is just a thirty-five minute ferry ride from the core of downtown Seattle. Given Seattle's tremendous traffic problem, the ferry commute is one of the best commutes if you live on the island and work downtown. As it turned out, most of the real estate available in my favorite neighborhood was way out of my reach, and I found a wonderful detached, three-story condo on the island, walking distance to the ferry. It was absolutely exhilarating to be back breathing the sweet ocean air and immersed in the all of the natural beauty of the Pacific Northwest. During the first weeks in my new home I vividly remember feeling a depth of gratitude that I had never tapped before. I was so happy to be home and immersed in the natural beauty that soothes my soul.

I was quite broken by the relationship that I had just left but could breathe easier once back home. Both the natural environment and the in-home environment in the area I had just returned from were not at all soothing for my soul. They were each cold as snot, with unpredictable raging storms, and became less attractive with each passing moment.

I had been living on the island for twenty months at the time that Jet was diagnosed. During the months leading up to his diagnosis, I had been waffling on whether or not I wanted to remain living on the island. I had acquired a good job a block away from my home but I was not enjoying the job at all. I was feeling the expense of taking a car across on the ferry to go and visit friends on the mainland. I was starting to feel the heavy weight of my mortgage and the unanticipated high cost of utilities and island living in general. Jet's diagnosis was the deciding factor for me to lease out my condo and return to Seattle, to be nearer to support Jet on his journey, and to provide my children with another place to lay their heads when they were in town to offer their love and support. I found a little apartment to rent, it was small but doable. I leased out my home on October 1, with the homeowner's association requirement that I lease for a minimum of one year. Now here is a perfect example of how life can just throw some crap; crap that's not supposed to break you, but just crap. I leased out my home on October 1, Jet went into the hospital the afternoon of October 3, and he died at 4:00 a.m. on October 5. It was so fast from diagnosis to death; fast, gut-wrenching, and heartbreaking. *Shit! Dammit! Aaagh!* Life just turned upside down for my children and me. When Jet died I wanted to *scream* at the top of my lungs, "Jet, your *Asshole!* How could you just up and die like that? Why didn't you let us know what the doctors had shared with you? Why did you push us away the last week of your life? *Aaagh!"*

As I sat at a little table on a quaint cobblestone street in the village, reflecting on the details of my environmental well-being, tears began streaming down my cheeks. Even though Jet had died eight months earlier, I hadn't even begun to process it. I had been in a "Be the glue, be the Executor, be the Trustee, be the beacon, be the only parent, be the damn everything to everyone" mode. The little place that I was living in, although cute and tidy on first appearance, turned out to be a very dark, cold, musty, and uncongenial environment to live in. My days were filled with handling the business of Jet's death, and working full-time hours on the Life Enrichment Team at a high end assisted-living facility. The hours were long and demanding and often involved working evenings and weekends. I was falling in love with many of the residents but was also feeling depleted of all energy by the end of the day.

I had only signed a six-month lease on the little apartment, with options to renew. I spent many hours in March and April looking for another place to rent for the five months that remained before I could return to my island home. Every second of every day was filled with the business of dying, my job, my crazy schedule, and looking for a place to lease for just five months. It was maddening. It was all too much. I didn't have any energy. I felt like I was just robotically making it through the days. My nights were engulfed with worry about how my children were faring after the loss of their father. And the constant dealings with the nitwits on the other end of the phone while conducting the business of Jet's death, felt endless and draining.

It was such an exhausting and fitful time. One morning, after being the victim of credit card fraud while going through the application process to lease a new place, I had an epiphany. It went something like this, "Just leave. Just pack the things you brought with you from your home and put them in storage. Quit the job that has promised to vet your education programs, but management has not followed through, and get on a damn plane to a faraway land. Just do it!" Oh my God, that thought felt so good in my body. And then that other voice, you know the discerning, scrutinizing, ugly stepsister voice, warned "How can you do that? Who do you think you are? Everybody would like to just pack and leave, but we don't get to do that. And how are you going to afford it anyway?" Right after saying *"Shut up"* to the ugly voice, I realized that I could actually do this. My children had received a little bit of money from a life insurance policy after their father died and my daughter had gifted some of it to me. As I was digesting these thoughts, a smile of possibility started to brew. From that moment on, during my only free hours between 11:00 p.m. and 2:00 a.m., I focused on researching places and programs that I could escape to for several months. The world is a big place so my beginning research was an enormous undertaking, until I scaled it down to Europe and to a focus on wellness. As you know on June 7, I split. Best decision *ever!*

As you can see the environmental piece of my well-being was out of whack. I was not living in a healthy space and not taking the time, or having any time to be immersed in nature. However, the most important thing to learn from this is how my thoughts were informing and guiding my story. Every day, at work and in my personal life, I was sharing my story of the dark, musty, damp, and cold environment that I was living in, the breathing problems it was causing me, the lack of sleep I was getting, and on and on. I was allowing the same focused thoughts and storytelling about my work environment too. The place was very high end but enormous and I would run about 15,000 to 20,000 steps a day, the hours were crazy, we were understaffed, overworked, and underpaid. Management had made promises about vetting programs and career opportunities that we were all starting to realize were never going to materialize. They cut staff from a variety of departments weekly and overworked the rest of us. Can you hear it, the heaviness, the ill-health, and the exhaustion from my own story? And I kept telling it. The crazy thing is I knew better! I have known better for a long time and yet I trapped myself in my own story. Why? *Who Am I*? How did I loose such sight of me?

One of the biggest decisions on my plate while on this sojourn was about my home. Should I move back into my home on the island? Should I let the mortgage and hefty expenses define my life and determine what I would need to earn to sustain my life? Should I allow the people leasing it to stay, since they have expressed that they would like to stay? In the big picture, should I keep it or sell it? If I sell it, where will I live, back in my favorite Seattle neighborhood? I do love it there but what about the cost? At the moment though, I just couldn't muster the focus to make these decisions. I was just starting to examine my story and begin the journey of untangling.

Whenever confronted by a tyrant, tormentor, teacher, friend, or foe (they all mean the same thing) remind yourself, "This moment is as it should be." Whatever relationships you have attracted in your life at this moment are precisely the ones you need in your life at this moment. There is a hidden meaning behind all events, and this hidden meaning is serving your own evolution.

Deepak Chopra

Chapter Four

Ahhhhh ------- Relationships!

Being present at the Shakti Center for twenty-one days plunked me right smack dab in the most healing, loving, nurturing environment. Breakfast, lunch, and dinner continued to be nutritious and delicious every single day. Panachakarma treatments were a gift and a blessing. I was starting to feel the healing and the release of toxins at deeper levels. I had a hint of feeling rested and had, during the second week, spent at least an hour or two a day walking around the village and contemplating how my thoughts had led me to such a place of despair in my life. Two evenings a week, I attended the yoga class taught by Amna. Several of the local village people attended the class, which was taught in German. I loved it. I couldn't understand a thing being said, but deep breathing is universal and I could see the yoga positions that I should be in. The class length was ninety minutes and I was always ready for sleep afterwards.

I had met a couple of women who had come to the Shakti Center for their own rest, nourishment, and healing. There was a woman leaving the first day that I arrived, who as I mentioned, was healing from the loss of her husband. Then there were about five days that only I was there. On day four, Sudeep, who I think was feeling a bit sorry for me, took me on a drive to a couple of neighboring villages. It was wonderful. A lot of the beauty in Germany is much like the forested, mountainous beauty of the Pacific Northwest. We drove on windy roads through rolling hills and the countryside. He took me to an amazing grocery store with fresh Ayurvedic herbs, and then to the "black and pink pig farm." That was fun. They are very proud of their meat products in Germany. On the way back we stopped on a country road and picked strawberries in a field. I looked up to the sky and smiled at God et al. and announced "I'm in a strawberry field in Germany with an Ayurvedic practitioner, and picking strawberries. *Who would have dreamt!*" Delicious, delicious, delicious; both the strawberries, and the moment. I felt blessed beyond belief.

On day five or six of being the only guest at the Shakti Center, a woman named Sophia came to stay for a week. She spoke some English and was an absolutely lovely lady. She too, had come to continue her healing after the loss of her husband. We made fast friends, and even though we were each immersed in our own healing, we did find time to take a few walks through the village. On a few hot summer evenings we went out to the old town square, and sipped cold drinks while we watched the theatre group practice on the stairs of an ancient cathedral. It was amazing, simply *amazing*. I don't know the name of the play they were rehearsing, but these highly skilled actors were performing as athletes playing a soccer game on the medieval and somewhat crumbling steps of the cathedral. There were moments that I was starting to truly have fun again. Not fake fun, nor exhausted laughter, but the real thing.

As the days passed, I continued my prayers to God, Brahman, Allah, Buddha, et al. And I continued to examine my thoughts and health in each area of my life. I also remained pretty frantically attached to my computer and the job boards, because I had just quit everything and walked away from life as I knew it. I definitely experienced moments of *freak out!* As so many of us know, trying to find work in this computerized age can be an overwhelming, impersonal, and arduous process. I was focused on healing, but I was also clinging to the thoughts of what I "should" be doing to make sure I could survive when I returned home.

After examining the environmental parts of my life and story, I turned my focus to the relational aspects. There is such a level of pathetic that, thank God, I can find hilarity and laugh at again. If I hadn't cut in the warped and demented humor line (twice) prior to my arrival in this incarnation, my life could have sucked in this category. And some of it is definitely not hilarious. Let's look at the thoughts guiding my relationship story. And I encourage you to do the same with the thoughts surrounding your relationship story.

During the second and third weeks at the Shakti Center, I continued to digest an enormous amount of nourishment, healing, and rest. As my mind-body was waking-up a bit, I think I was most struck by the rawness of my feelings over Jet's death. We had divorced twenty-six years earlier, when our children were just four and eleven years old. As I have shared, we had continued a close friendship for over two decades, celebrating each of our birthdays, holidays and other special events together as a family. In the early years, I was convinced that I was earning my angel wings by maintaining our friendship and by being the greatest advocate of sharing family celebrations. I do know there had to be profound value in that because our children, as they grew up, came to each of us on occasion and thanked us for never having to be worried to have their parents present in the same room, or at the same celebration. They had seen what some of their friends had to go through and it wasn't pretty. So there was goodness in our choice. However, over the years those choices also continued to put me in a situation where my children saw me treated in ways that I did not deserve. And I tolerated it. I did not want to make our family gatherings uncomfortable, so I withstood treatment like being silenced if I wanted to contribute to a conversation, or ridiculed for my interests and passions. It was a double-edged sword. Jet had extremely lovely qualities, *and* he was also proud to be an asshole at times. For ten years after our divorce, Jet could have had his family back. It was deeply sad to me that he either could not, or would not choose health, well-being, and a shared family life.

I also want to highlight the good that came to all of us from our choices and our enduring friendship. Jet was a huge presence in life, and larger than life in so many ways, especially in his own mind. I say that with a smile. He was charismatic, charming, and quick-witted. He had a brilliant legal mind and he loved his work. We benefited from his love, his generosity, his gracious spirit, his grandeur, his financial success, and his connections. Our children are well traveled; they have stayed in some of the finest hotels, and have experienced many wonderful events that most people never get to experience. Jet was an amazing host and he loved to entertain. He lived large. I think that his conscious evolution was a bit blocked by a focus on ego. He was so attached to the things that feed ego: his job title, his possessions, his elite air mile status, the money he earned, and the connections he had. You know what I'm talking about, the things that this hypnosis of society has taught us to value, and to so dearly cling to.

Jet was an easy and hard man to love. We enjoyed each other's quick-witted humor, and we were a dynamic professional duo, a true force to be reckoned with. We laughed easily and often. I wish we would have made it together *and* I am grateful that we didn't. I am shocked by how huge an absence I have been experiencing since he died. He was an enormous footprint on my life and in my heart. There were also times along the way that our parenting philosophies crashed up against each other, and times when his constant coming and going when we were married hurt our family so much. I do feel his absence. I see and feel the pain and loss that our children are suffering. I feel this enormous absence from my own life. I feel two ways about that absence. First and foremost, I feel the loss of my friend and our shared history; and I feel the relief of not being poked at. I think that many of us experience this type of relief when someone dies, if their behavior at times was less than honorable. I also think that we silence these feelings when it might be more beneficial to express and heal them. I found myself thinking that with Jet's death, some of the ill-treatment I have received in my life had finally died. But on deeper introspection, I was realizing that there were shadow aspects of me that I needed to examine, heal, and put to rest.

So in those first weeks of my sojourn, I was experiencing a combination of sadness, a sense of feeling lost, and absolute disbelief that Jet was gone. And as his Executor, I had been living and breathing his death every day for the preceding eight months. My days were consumed with reporting his death to the appropriate agencies, sending death certificates and Letters Testamentary to dozens and dozens of people so they could talk with me and help me wrap up business; and dealing with the nitwits, the endless number of nitwits. I should have kept a log of the emotional retardation that I encountered. At least at the end of the worst conversations, I had developed the ability to laugh at the folly of it all. There is one though that stands out above the rest. It was just weeks ago that I received a call from a large pharmaceutical company. When I answered the telephone a man said, "Hello, this is _____ Pharmacies calling for Mr. Hawks." I said "He is deceased," and the young man replied, "Oh well, I was just calling to update his contact information, but hey since he's dead and I have you on the phone Ma'am, are you experiencing any pain or discomfort and are your medications working for you?" Enough time had passed that out of my mouth came the words, "Oh no, no pain felt here. It's just death. I don't think we need to make a big thing out of it. Now you have a nice day. *Asshole!* I hope this call is on a recorded line!"

Speaking of assholes, I will move on to discuss another significant relationship. Yes, with the man on the handsome steed. During my first week of panchakarma in Schwabisch Hall, I was consciously intending to get the rest of my feelings and thoughts about this man exorcised from my Being. My mantra was a very loud *"Please help me heal"* from this bang-up experience. Now, I am the first person to forgive everybody of everything as soon as possible. And I had been forgiving him, but man oh man, the pain hung on and the pain was an indicator to me that I had a deeper level of forgiveness to experience. This man still held a strong presence in the story I was living out loud. I kept thinking about the experience. I kept trying to understand it, and in an attempt to make sense of it I kept sharing it out loud with friends and family.

From the time that Jet and I divorced, and until the man on the handsome steed, I had dated over the years but not a lot. For the first fifteen years, I was very focused on raising our children, and Jet was holding a significant place in our lives and in our hearts. I dated here and there for three to six months at a time, but no one that I felt like inviting into our lives. And then along came the galloping man.

I will keep this as short and as sweet as I can. I was totally smitten but not entirely thrilled with the thought of relocating. I had the blessings of my children, who had their own level of discomfort with me leaving, but who were so supportive because they saw how happy I was. He had swept me off my feet. This man said that he found me stunning, gorgeous, intelligent, funny, and sexy. He couldn't wait to see me next, and we spent endless hours talking and laughing on the telephone. I mean split-your-gut laughing. The clincher for me was when he spoke the words, "Let me take care of you. For the first time in your life, just lean in and let me take care of you. You can keep your place in Seattle and I'll cover all of the expenses. I'll fly you home to see your kids and friends every month. Our life together is going to be filled with friends. We'll always have a weekly night out together. And our retirement is absolutely secure. I don't want you to work. I want you to take the time to write that you have been talking about. We will spend a year in my city but we will invest in a home and always have a Seattle presence. I don't care about staying in my city at all. We will spend most of our time here in Seattle." *Sold!* I was over the moon. I couldn't believe this was finally happening to me. The great love that I had known and believed was going to show up in my life, did. I found him to be very attractive, light hearted, engaging, an excellent listener, and oh how we laughed. So I packed-up, sold many possessions, and left others with my daughter for my return. I did not keep the place I was leasing or the associated costs because I thought the expense would be a burden on this gracious man. Suffice it to say, I was very new to "leaning" in.

After I had relocated and had been in his home for about eight days, I said to the galloping man, "What did you do, get the girl and now you're letting your true self out?" And I laughed. What I was about to learn was that no truer statement had ever been spoken. From the moment I arrived, he walked differently, he talked differently, and over the next several months I was starting to witness incongruences between his verbal and nonverbal behavior. The man was a chameleon. I saw him become whatever the situation lent itself too. He selected other people's words and made them his own. It was seven months before I ever met a single one of his friends. He announced to me one day that he had enough friends in his friendship network, and that I was not to pursue any of my own. I was informed that our weekly night out was a "man's night out" and that I was not invited.

Eventually the lies started to show themselves on a regular basis. On occasion, he would break into a rage from nowhere, in our home and at times in public, typically after we had been out with friends and I had had a good time. He attempted to reduce me to a complete sex object. He no longer treated me like a human being, I was an "it". He would say, "Bring it over here," and bring "it" dressed in black stockings because "I like what I like." I found it all very disturbingly offensive. I think that Jennifer Aniston's line on an episode of *Friends*, best captures the feelings I was experiencing about my predicament. She said "Now isn't that just kick you in the crouch, spit on your neck fantastic!"

During the first year, I was blindsided again and again. After that, I was just trying to figure out how to get home safe and with my possessions. I know that so many of us have been hurt and disappointed in love. For me, this hurt was overwhelming at many levels. It wasn't just the shock of being so swept off of my feet and deceived; more than anything else, I was so unbelievably disappointed in myself for not seeing him for who he really was. For a long time I experienced that level of disappointment in myself. I couldn't get my head around it. At the time this man came into my life, I had been meditating for fifteen years. I had been teaching meditation for fourteen years. I had been studying and consciously evolving for thirty years. I never saw him coming. In her book, *Dodging Energy Vampires*, Dr. Christiane Northrup shares, "I couldn't imagine that there were people who are nearly devoid of empathy, compassion, caring, and the willingness or even capacity to change. But this is exactly what energy vampires are. They are chameleons who can be master manipulators, getting what they want from others without giving anything in return."

One of my first healing acts on this sojourn was to consciously release any of the hurt, memories, and shit from that relationship. During several of my initial panchakarma treatment sessions, I held an *unbending intention* to let it all out, and I did. My feelings spilled out in the form of deep sighs, gasps for air, and streaming tears. It was extremely freeing and phenomenally healing. And I'm happy to report that since day twenty-seven of this sojourn, I have been free of that experience at a cellular level. I forgave at a profound level. I have always known that forgiving frees our own hearts, and that the person we are forgiving doesn't need to deserve it, or even know that we are consciously performing that act of grace. However, it has been a challenge for me throughout my life, to forgive myself. I now see the galloping man, as the petty tyrant and teacher, who helped me to learn the deep, deep lesson of self-forgiveness. Don't go crazy on me. I didn't send him a thank-you card, but I have thanked the *Universe* for the awareness and the ability to forgive myself. How did I forgive myself? By holding the same *unbending* intention to allow only loving, accepting, honoring, and forgiving thoughts about myself to enter my mind. It takes sheer determination and practice but the outcome is absolutely worth it.

Upon examining these significant relationships in my life, I was beginning to see that energy vampires have had a presence in my life since I arrived on this planet. Dr. Northrup also spells out, in detail, how energy vampires can have a devastating effect on the people they seek out. She states that they, "Feed on the life force of others," and that they fall somewhere on a continuum of less severe to extremely severe. Where Jet, had a dollop of asshole mixed with a splash of narcissism all rolled up in a kind and empathic batter, he was not an energy vampire. The man on the handsome steed, I believe, was on the severe end of the continuum. I think my angels had hoped that I would examine a shadow aspect of myself, with just a dollop and a splash in a love relationship experience. But no, I walked head on into the zinger relationship that would leave me almost broken.

I spent several deeply introspective evenings wandering around the village, and examining my relationships with the energy vampires in my life. In my younger years the energy vampire was a parental figure. As a result of this influence in my life, I was starting to see how I had attracted relationships by allowing a shadow part of me to have a voice. And I was becoming aware, that the death of another person, or the death of a relationship, would not end the ill-treatment I have received. I was realizing that there was another death that needed to happen. The death of the voice that I had given to a shadow aspect of myself, which had convinced me, that I was not completely loved and completely lovable. Yes my dears, the death of something that I had given voice to. This awareness will completely change my life and my love story. And that, my friends, is an example of what I refer to as *awarefulness!* (Except for that little end-zone dance that I just busted out, that was all Ego!) We cannot heal a damn thing, until we bring it to our awareness and have the courage to look in the mirror and own it.

The path to enlightenment includes not only
the search for the divine but also the total
acceptance of the shadow self.

Deepak Chopra

Chapter Five

Woman in the Mirror

I t was now my third week in Schwabisch Hall and I continued
to enjoy my walks around the village. Many of the shopkeepers,
waiters, waitresses, and villagers had come to recognize me.
I was beginning to feel like a local, albeit an illiterate local. I had
never traveled like this with so much time in one place. I *can* tell
you, that it's just outstanding. I was also spending a great deal of
time that week researching where to go next. I loved my time in
this sweet little village, but my twenty-one days would be over
soon, too soon. I had tentative plans to meet a dear friend and her
son, who is my age, in Paris the following week. However, she had
not been well the past few weeks, and it looked like I might need
to make another plan.

As I wandered around on the cobblestone streets, past the beer
gardens, and across covered bridges over the river that meanders
through the village, I reflected deeply on my story. I have had a
practice in place since I was twenty-eight years old that I have used
as a checkpoint in my life. Regardless of what I am going through,
whether it is a job, or a relationship, or a difficult time, I ask myself
these questions: "What is the gift in this situation? What is the
lesson? How is this petty tyrant a teacher? Do I see a reflection of

myself in this other person? Do I see shadows of me in the other? Have I forgiven anyone that has misled or mistreated me? Who Am I? Why Am I? What about me attracted this situation into my life? What frequency are my thoughts and my story vibrating to?"

It's a very nice little check system that asks us to become self-aware, or as I prefer to say, consciously pursuing a journey to *awarefulness*. A self-examination process is simply the best habit we can develop on our path to consciously evolving. I actually think that it is the only way to evolve, and ultimately, to attain enlightenment. Let me elaborate a bit about how this process works. I'll use my relationship with the man on the handsome steed as an example. What was the gift in this situation? I had the opportunity to spend some time with my father who was just an hour's flight away. I had the opportunity to visit with him in his own home and with his wife. I got to know their two children. I came to love my brother, his wife, and their two sons very, very much. That is a forever gift and I am deeply grateful. I also received the gift of awareness that I no longer needed to romanticize that side of the family. They are just people. They have a family system that most seem content with. Nobody calls anybody out on anything. Emotions are swept under carpets and tucked away. Everything is sustained at a jovial surface level. Imagine what a shock to the family system "live-out-loud" I was. I love. I feel. I ask questions. I share freely about who I am and what jazzes my soul. I have a genuine interest in getting to know people. I call people out on their crap and expect the same courtesy in return. Gently, and in nice ways, but I do call them out. For example, by gently I mean, if my grown children sat around our dining room table and treated anyone with the disrespect that I observed between and among a few family members I would leap across the table, grab them by the scruff of their necks, and gently flip them out the front door. I can't actually imagine doing that with my children because we have a code of honor and respect in place in our lives. But could I do it? Heck yes! Maybe my "live-out-loud" scared these people!

What is the lesson? And how is the petty tyrant a teacher? Self-forgiveness is the lesson. I had never walked so blindly into a situation in the years since I have been consciously evolving. I think the intensity of the situation with the galloping man was obviously necessary for me to learn the depth of self-forgiveness. And in those acts of self-forgiveness, I have also metabolized a level of grace that had previously eluded me. I have always been a seeker of wisdom and grace. Careful what you ask for! The *Universe* will surely bless you with the opportunity to learn.

Do I see a reflection of myself in this other person? Do I see shadows of me? I think it has been at least a decade or so since I attended a Seduction of Spirit seminar, where Deepak walked us through a divine type of self-questioning. He pointed out that those qualities and characteristics that we see so easily in others, especially the ones we find distasteful, is because they are familiar to us within our own selves. This is huge! It is more than saying that "it takes two to tangle." This self-examination process asks us to look at things we may not want to see. It asks us to become aware of and to examine our shadow side. For example, when I say that the galloping man reduced me to an object, which he did, the higher question is "How have I reduced *Who I Am* to an object?" Are there areas in my life where I am strongly identifying *Who I Am* as a "skin encapsulated ego?" Am I looking in the mirror and criticizing this body, its wrinkles, its imperfections, its age? Yes, prior to becoming more aware, I have certainly spent mirror-time criticizing this body, its wrinkles, its blemishes, its belly-fat, its graying hair, and drooping breasts; instead of embracing the miracle that I am. Did I present myself primarily as a sex object? That's a big no, but I must admit it was really a great feeling to have someone so physically attracted to me. When the man on the handsome steed was yelling and screaming and I felt the terror in my soul, does that ability to terrorize exist within me? The answer is yes, the possibility does exist. It is something that I do? No. Is it something that I am capable of doing? Yes. What about me attracted this relationship into my life? What frequencies were my thoughts, mind, and body resonating to?

With the galloping man, it all happened so fast and the relationship blossomed at a twenty-five-hundred-mile distance. I'd like to think that I would have tapped into things quicker, and without disrupting my life so much, had we been in the same city as our relationship developed. I definitely would have seen the verbal and nonverbal incongruence sooner. I think some of the frequencies that I was vibrating to were born, in part, as a result of letting go of my late afternoon meditation and instead filling the space with a glass or two of wine. As my move approached, I remember sitting at an outdoor café in Seattle with this man, and sharing with him that I am keenly aware of when my mind and body feel aligned and well. I told him that day that I felt like my alignment wasn't an "Inch off, but across the street off." I kept prodding him for clarity about our situation, and that everything was genuine and honest. He assured me that everything was absolutely genuine and "transparent." It was about four weeks later that I ruptured a disk in my lower back. I felt dropped to my knees, crippled in pain. I had had lower back surgery seventeen years earlier, and had learned how to live a pain-free, healthy-back lifestyle, through yoga, walking, meditation, aquafit, and vibrating to higher frequencies. My body was screaming at me to take heed. It had given me a huge red flag. I was not yet making the connections. So my angels tried harder.

During the month that I injured my back I went to see an acupuncturist in hopes that it would help me avoid another back surgery. Very long story short, I ended up having lower back surgery, and at the six-week post-op appointment I was still experiencing an intense, hot, nerve-like pain in my left foot, and asked my neurosurgeon if that pain was nerve damage that I had to live with. At that time, he was able to determine that the particular area of pain in my foot was unrelated to the disk and nerves in question. An x-ray revealed that there had been a broken acupuncture needle in my foot for the past two-and-a-half months. Hence the horrible burning pain. The needle had fractured a bone in my foot, and two weeks later I had foot surgery to remove the fractured bone. So here you go. Now I'd had back surgery and a few months later, foot surgery, and was wearing a protective boot and walking with crutches. Four days after surgery I boarded my flight to go be with the galloping man.

Oh my, saying it all out loud like this makes me want to both laugh and cry. As you know, I pray to God et al. regularly and I ask my angels for guidance every day. Well, it seems that my angels were doing just about everything in their power to get my attention, including carrying those huge clubs that they'd been forced to hit me over the head with. I think my angels always start with a little whisper, and then get louder and a bit louder even. Then they bring out the clubs. I can actually remember lying on my living room floor after both surgeries and asking my angels "Is this a sign that I should stay put and not move away to be with this man?" Oh my, oh my. Of course it was. But tootle on I did. You've heard the story.

Being able to release the heartache and trauma of that relationship during panchakarma treatments was just excellent. Examining aspects of my story was equally excellent. And I continued to do so.

I next looked at my physical well-being. I am fifty-nine years old and I have always led a very fit and active lifestyle. However, during the last two years since I entered menopause, I have also packed on ten pounds contributing to a bit of a wiggly- jiggly middle quadrant of my body. Years ago, after overhearing a conversation between two middle-aged women who were discussing their mutual dislike of their "muffin-tops," I was left wondering, "What the hell is a muffin-top?" Well, I wonder no more. I resisted these changes to my body's new shape for the first year, until it occurred to me to love this vessel that provides a life presence for my soul. It is a very strange experience to be carrying extra pounds. I have been able to maintain my college weight throughout my adult life. I am attributing my late entry into menopause and my weight gain to that previous life as an axe murderer thing again. What was I thinking? *Truly*. I remember Deepak saying, "If you want to know what your thoughts have been like up until now, examine your body today; and if you want to know what your body will look like in the years to come, examine your thoughts today." So, yes menopause is a huge transformation and hormonal shift, but how had my thoughts influenced this process?

Reflecting back I realized that I had not only had a lot of stress for the past several years resulting in a broken heart; but also, I had had nearly a decade of stress leading up to that time watching someone I love dearly struggle with a dis-ease. During the latter part of that decade I had also taken to drinking red wine, several glasses, several times a week. I don't even like wine but I liked the buzz and the numbing effect. It took the edge off and it also packed on some pounds. I continued reflecting back on how these choices heightened my scrutiny of me and my disappointment in myself. I was well aware that I was imbibing in a toxic substance, having toxic thoughts, and feeling high levels of stress and helplessness. And I was resonating to a much lower frequency when I did so. To me, this definitely explains how I would attract an unhealthy relationship. That seems to go hand in hand when we abuse our relationship with ourselves. Low frequency substances and low frequency thinking attract low frequency relationships. It all makes sense. Deepak states "That we attract into our lives who we are" at any given moment.

Let me say a little more about what I mean by low frequencies. Anything that weakens us is a low frequency. Toxic substances, toxic environments, and toxic thoughts and feelings like shame, guilt, anger, humiliation, judgement, and negative beliefs are all low frequencies. In his book, *The Biology of Belief*, Dr. Bruce Lipton states that "Our positive and negative beliefs not only impact our health, but also every aspect of our life." Wayne Dyer and Deepak Chopra have written and spoken at length about how our thoughts are the determining factors in our overall well-being, and the quality of our lives.

When I wasn't spending time deeply reflecting on my life, I was spending time during the evenings at the Shakti Center researching a backup travel plan if my dear friend was not able to meet me in Paris. I had six weeks to fill in, between the time I would leave Schwabisch Hall and the time I would arrive in Poland, where I was to stay for my last twenty-eight days. I also had tentative plans to meet a friend in Amsterdam and then travel on to Prague during weeks five and six. I was starting to feel a little panicky because I had no updates from my friend on our Paris plan, and all of the good deals that I was researching were being bought up at lightning speed.

I finally heard confirmation from my friend, through her son, that they were going to postpone their trip until she felt much stronger. I was surprised at the relief that I felt. I had been really looking forward to Paris. When I sat quietly with myself and pondered the feeling of relief, I realized two things. First, Paris was going to cost more than I had hoped to spend on any given week during my travels. But more than that, the deeper feeling of relief, was that without Paris and without hooking up with friends at that time, I could stay the course of my deep self-reflective work and healing. That was just an outstanding feeling. I did not want to veer off my path.

You overcome old habits by leaving them behind.

Wayne Dyer

Chapter Six

Waking-Up from my Waking State

With twenty-one days of deep rest, healing, and nourishment under my belt, I was searching for a place to wake-up and reenergize. I wanted to stay out of countries on the euro, but took a peek at a few anyway, and I wanted to stay for another twenty-one days. That is a long time in one place, but it had been absolutely magical to have that amount of time in Schwabisch Hall, and I wanted more of that! I peeked at places in Southern France and Italy. France was very intriguing but way over my budget for a twenty-one day stay. I found some wonderful deals in Italy, but I have never enjoyed traveling solo in Italy. There is this feeling of having to be hypervigilant and that is not what I was seeking. Croatia was on the top of my list but so many of the great deals had already been grabbed up. I also explored Slovakia and Slovenia. I wanted to be immersed in history and surrounded by natural beauty; somewhere I could walk until my feet screamed. And I wanted aquafit classes and a little gym where I could jumpstart the slumped state that I had been in for months prior to my departure. I was also looking for ease of travel from my chosen destination to Amsterdam, where I would meet my friend Adara from Seattle, who was scheduled to join me.

Have you ever found that sometimes life would be so much easier if there were only ten choices? Or better yet, two! I was feeling the intensity of not having decided where to go next and finally just chose. It was such a *relief!* I chose Croatia and then *"unchose"* Croatia. It had been a particularly hot week in Schwabisch Hall, and when I focused on the weather forecast in Croatia for the next weeks, I decided I would burn up and die. I adore the sunshine and blue skies but I do not adore heat. Seventy-five degrees is about my perfect sunny weather day. Then I chose a little village in Bavaria, Bad Wörishofen. Then I *"unchose"* it. And then I chose Marienbad in the Czech Republic. On July 5, I departed Schwabisch Hall on a train bound to Marienbad via Nuremburg and Cheb.

I had learned that Marienbad (Mariánské Lázně) was a spa town in West Bohemia, Czech Republic. I spoke with my booking representative, and after listening to all of my woes about where to go next, she told me that I could not go wrong with Marienbad. She said that it was located in the spa triangle and that the area attracted Russian and German people for health and wellness vacations. She continued to share that it is also known for its curative carbon dioxide springs, and that it was absolutely gorgeous.

It fit the bill and was amazingly cost effective. Three train rides and I would be smack dab in the middle of the spa triangle. I was excited and thrilled. I am well-traveled enough to know how to pack light and travel light. However, for this sojourn I was traveling with a larger and heavier case than normal. I brought full size shampoos, conditioners, moisturizers, and a thousand-pack box of condoms, just in case I had the opportunity to test the effectiveness of my kegel muscle workouts. I am teasing about the thousand-pack of condoms, it was more like eight hundred. *I'm joking, I'm joking.* I think I had one forty-year-old condom melted to an inside pocket of my suitcase somewhere. I was also carrying my laptop, together with wireless keyboard and mouse, in my backpack. I opted for a backpack instead of my leather business case on wheels so I could have my hands free to lift my heavy case off and on trains. My only solace was that my case would (or should) be getting lighter each passing week, and I was going to donate my backpack and pick up a small carry-on with wheels after my train travel was completed. It was a good plan.

It was bittersweet saying goodbye to Sudeep, Amna and Rathi. They all brought deep healing, cleansing, nourishment, and life back into me. I was wearing that signature smile of mine again. I was starting to remember *who I am.* After big hugs and lots of expressed gratitude, Sudeep drove me to the train station. Thank goodness, because this particular station had many, many steps down to the platform and no elevator or moving belt that runs along the stairs for your cases. He carried my heavy case and backpack down three flights of stairs, and expressed his concern that I was going to hurt myself, and undo some of the magical healing that I had just received. I promised him I would take care of myself.

The first train was a regional train and I was a little disappointed with how modern it was. No old private cabins in any of the cars. You know the kind of old train cars that fantasies are born of. I had a first class ticket and there was only me and one gentleman in that section. I fantasized about him anyway! Why not? He was mysterious and quite attractive. He was dressed in a dark blue business suit with a crisp white shirt and thin burgundy colored tie. I was trying to imagine what accent I would hear as he whispered his desires in my ear. He had dark hair, sea-blue eyes, high cheek bones, a chiseled chin, and an alluring smile; very dreamy indeed. I spent the entire train ride sheepishly glancing his way; and then looking out the window and playing with the idea that this handsome man might be a lovely, intelligent, available soul, and that we'd experience this kismet kind of soul connection. I watched the scenery out the window and imagined a shared life together. He was a widower, with grown children. They lived about an hour's drive away from the cottage that he and I had just purchased in a charming village near the German Alps. He spoke a little English and I was becoming fluent in German. My children visited us for month-long stays each year. He traveled with me to the Pacific Northwest twice a year. It was a beautiful life. We enjoyed a decade together before he fell ill with an unknown auto-immune disease. As his condition weakened, his children started to express their strong opinions that everything should be left to them in his Will, including our sweet home. My children didn't want me to be so far away playing the role of caregiver. I was feeling torn about what to do given the gravity of the situation.

The conductor announced that our next stop was Nuremburg. And I laughed out loud at the fact that this handsome man and I had barely even made eye contact, and I had played out a fantasy life together right down to his demise. We women are quite amusing that way.

The train ride to Nuremburg was about two hours and I had planned it so I could have a ninety-minute layover between trains. I figured the possibility existed that it could take me ninety minutes just to maneuver the stairs up and down between platforms. Nuremburg, however, was a very impressive station. It was extremely modern with all of the necessary lifts and superb shops and restaurants. Now, as you all know I had just eaten the most nourishing Ayurvedic healing meals for twenty-one straight days. What did I order for my meal between trains? I ordered a large pretzel and a large German beer. *Outstanding!* I figured there was no better time to run amuck with my eating than that day. How much harm could I do with such a clean start? I enjoyed every single bite of that pretzel and every single sip of that delicious beer.

Catching my train from Nuremberg to Cheb was a bit of a challenge. I went to the correct platform, and there were two signs lit for two trains departing at the same time, from the same platform. I was really confused. I never panic at things like that because my feeling is if I get on the wrong train, oh well, then I end up there. Maybe that's where I was supposed to end up; or I catch a next train back. Again, I was surrounded by non-English speaking people. Then, seeing the confusion on my face, a lovely gentleman approached me and in very broken English told me that this one train does go to both places, that it "splits" at one of the stops so I need to make sure that I am on the right part of the train going to Cheb, and not the part of the train splitting off and going somewhere else. *Who knew!* I boarded the train and when the conductor came through I confirmed that I was on the part of the train going to Cheb. In Cheb, I would change to a local train heading to Marienbad. The train station in Cheb was very confusing. My train wasn't listed on any of the boards. I walked up and down the stairs to all six platforms but could not find my train, which was scheduled to depart in ten minutes. I finally went upstairs and out to the street. I saw a bus that said "Marienbad" on the front window. When I showed the bus driver my ticket, he closed the door on me, and then pointed through the window to a small separate train platform. I made that connection and arrived in Marienbad in the early evening. From the station I would take a taxi to the Velkolepý Hotel.

I assumed that there would be taxis at the train station, but I was wrong. You have to call for a taxi. I was certainly not making any calls on my cell phone, which remained in airplane-mode for the duration of my trip. The train station in Cheb was very small and I had difficulty finding someone to help me call for a taxi. Finally, the shopkeeper of the newsstand and candy shop, walked up to me and pantomimed that he could call the taxi for me. I was delighted to be rescued. I was feeling the long day of travel and the burden of toting my cases at that particular moment, and just wanted to get to the hotel. Twenty minutes later I was checking in at the Velkolepý Hotel. It was only a few kilometers from the train station.

The ride from the train station was quick and the scenery was beautiful. Marienbad did not disappoint. It looked just like the Google Images that I had pulled up on my laptop several days earlier. The city was surrounded with forested hillsides and was gorgeously green, much like the Pacific Northwest. The architecture was just outstanding. It looked almost gothic. There were dozens of hotels circling what must have been one hundred acres of parkland. The hotels all offered spa services and were immensely grand. I felt totally transported back in time, and in a crazy way everything also felt familiar, except of course, the language.

As I was checking in at the Velkolepý Hotel, I had my very first experience of the cultural lack of interpersonal communication skills and what I can only describe as "annoyed" that I was there. I did my normal charade-type communication and showed my paperwork. I always carried two sets of paperwork for each place that I stayed, one in the native language of the country, and one in English. Only the hotel's general manager spoke some English. After I had settled into my room I ventured out to explore the hotel and found my way to the lounge. The general manager found me there, and took a minute to let me know that he was "disappointed" to tell me that it is not likely that I would encounter any English speakers. I was actually delighted to hear that. I adored being steeped in the foreignness of it all. He shared with me the procedures for dining. For the duration of my trip, I purposefully stayed at places offering "full-board," meaning that the package price included all of my meals and I made sure to also include exercise programs. The procedures for dining were, "The dining hall is downstairs next to the spa area. You can sit at any table for breakfast and lunch but for dinner you will have an assigned table that you must sit at every night." I wasn't sure I was tickled about the assigned table for evening dinners but was fairly certain that I would meet some characters. And in all likelihood, since I was staying for twenty-one days, my dining partners would be changing week by week.

It was a hot summer evening, and outside the lounge was an upper patio overlooking the pool. I went and sat at a table on the patio and ordered a drink. I can't remember if I ordered a gin and tonic or what? But I can tell you that it was the first of the very few drinks that I would order over the course of twenty-one days, and it smacked of horrible. I couldn't identify what was in it. I carried my water bottle with me everywhere after that experience. I think it was sometime during week two that I got brave and ordered a tonic water, because I figured it was a shot at something they could not screw up. I was completely wrong about that. They served me something with some kind of alcohol in it. *Such a delightful adventure I am on.* And how arrogant do the above sentences sound. You know, the Ugly American who wants things exactly the way that they are at home, or in my case the Ugly Canadian. Truth be told, I think both my mind and body were rejecting any alcoholic beverages. I have actually never enjoyed hard alcohol. It just gives me the sugary shakes. I am also certain that after detoxing with panchakarma, my body was not willing to intake any more toxins.

I had missed all of the mealtimes on my arrival day at Velkolepý. So I went for a walk and found a little corner grocer, and bought a box of what from the photo looked like cheese crackers, and I found a spread for the crackers on the next aisle. The crackers were splendid and hit the spot. The spread may have been brill cream. It was a good partner to the drink I had.

Before going to bed the first night, I walked around the entire hotel specifically searching out information on their aquafit and Nordic walking classes. That was an essential component in choosing this hotel. I had been detoxed, nourished, and rested at the Shakti Center and I was now in phase two of my grand plan, to wake-up and get some energy back. I saw that they had aquafit classes every weekday morning and it looked like Nordic walking was also offered each afternoon. There was a gorgeous courtyard with both indoor and outdoor pools, and a very fancy spa area. I think that I have shared with you that Marienbad attracts wealthy German and Russian people for healing holidays every year. Now I was surrounded by the sound of German, Russian, and Czech languages. *How much fun is this!*

I unpacked my case and settled in for the evening. I was up early the next morning and went downstairs to the dining hall to eat. This was my first meal, of three buffet-style meals a day, for twenty-one days. It was a very impressive set-up and enjoyable food choices. That was my day one experience.

Aquafit classes were scheduled to start at 9:00 a.m. I made sure that I was in the pool all set to go at 8:45 a.m. 9:00 a.m. came, 9:05, 9:10, and finally at 9:15 the thirty- minute class started. Our instructor spoke Czech, and enough Russian and German to engage all of the participants. I simply adored not being able to understand a single word. Our dear teacher, who I would guess was in his early to mid-thirties, wore very tight, little, athletic shorts, and from my angle looking up from the water, they were not the best choice if he wanted to retain any element of confidentiality about what he was sporting down there. Maybe I was the only one that was gawking and fighting back a shit-eating grin. Everyone else in the pool was at least the age of my parents. I assume they either couldn't see that kind of detail, or had forgotten to bother looking. Having worked in a retirement community setting, I was much more concerned about all of the peeing in the pool. Not that anyone other than me was doing that.

I was taking in the whole experience and trying to follow what the instructor was saying; and when I couldn't understand his pool side instruction, there was always a gentleman (or two) that was happy to show me what my feet should be doing underwater. I was able to hold back the laughter that had been brewing inside of me from the start of the class, *until* our instructor started marching and moving his hips in this little wiggle and saying *"p'shhh, p'shhh, p'shhh, p'shhh."* I was bursting at the seams. It was all so deliciously entertaining. Class ended exactly at the thirty-minute point from when it should have started; another cultural nuance. It appeared that there was no concern about starting the class on time, but it did end on time.

Oh, and there was Hans. I met Hans the first day of class. He was German and spoke a little bit of English. He was a talker! Hans and his wife, about twelve years my senior, had come for healing spa treatments. She suffered with some type of illness. He told me of the "gas injections" his wife was receiving, which I learned were a common practice in some of the spa-treatment facilities. I can't tell you much about them because nobody spoke enough English to explain them to me. I simply knew that I did not want any. Hans said he thought they were a placebo. Maybe so. Maybe so. I did not include any treatments in the package I chose for my stay in Marienbad. I didn't want to screw up any of the health benefits I was experiencing from my twenty-one days of panchakarma.

After the first couple of days, I was finding my rhythm and routine. I would go to the spa area first thing in the morning. The waiting areas were filled with men and women, clad in thick white robes, waiting for their pre-arranged spa treatment, massage, and whatever else the menu board said. I would go into the little gym and ride the exercise bike until I was dripping sweat. That took all of about eight minutes. Next, I hopped on to the elliptical-type machine for fifteen minutes, and then I would go to the yoga room next door and do floor exercises and stretches. Then off to breakfast, followed by anywhere from twelve to eighteen minutes of aquafit, which worked essentially to get my cheek muscles in shape from holding back the insane amount of laughter I felt inside. I was far from feeling energized during the first week, but I could feel my energy waking-up. In the afternoons I would enjoy long walks in the park.

There was a very tall and stern Russian man that I would see most mornings in the little gym. He would look at me but never respond when I said hello. Actually, I had learned to say "hallo" with an accent I can't really describe. I felt like I was in a "man's gym" and that no woman should be there. But I truly didn't give a rip. Every morning he was there and I would smile and say "hallo." No smile, no nothing in return. Until the end of the week when he was preparing to leave (most people came for a week or ten days) and he came up to me, patted my arm, and gave me a huge smile. It made my day. I felt like I was in that scene in the movie *Under the Tuscan Sun,* where Diane Lane has regularly observed this older gentleman from her balcony. He is outside on the street placing flowers on what looked like a memorial wall, and he would make eye contact but never smile. Until the end of the movie, when he looks up at her, tips his hat, and smiles. It was such a sweet feeling.

During my quiet contemplative walks in the park, I continued to examine my life and my story, and say my prayers to God, Brahman, Allah, Buddha, Krishna, et al., you know the clan. The park was huge with a smell of ancient in the air. It was vast, with areas sporting artist sculptures carved in rock, some arising up out of ponds, and a whistling fountain, an exquisite promenade, and little cafes with cakes, pickled things, and refreshing beverages. Moms and dads watched as little children ran through the play areas. I was immersed in so much life, and after long walks I would sit, watch and enjoy, and at times break down in tears healing the heaviness in my heart. There were also out loud laughs at kids being kids. You can change countries and languages, but you cannot change kids just being kids. They kick and spit and throw tantrums and poop themselves about the same way in any language. *Absolutely delicious!*

Your thoughts do not belong to you, and once you understand that, then you can be the author of your destiny.

Deepak Chopra

Chapter Seven

The Hypnosis

I sat in the park, and while watching the children, I also reflected on a moment of instant awakening, a *Satori,* that I had experienced right before leaving Schwabisch Hall. For me these moments are so profound. I catch a glimpse of an understanding that is deep and elusive, and has an energy about it that soothes me at a soul level. These are fleeting moments and I find myself gripping to hang on to them. At a deeper level, I know that they have shown themselves to me for my own exploration, conscious evolution, and to experience a taste of enlightenment. As I develop my understanding and can wrap words around a level of awareness that is almost indescribable, and begin to metabolize the understanding, then I can begin to articulate what I was shown. In his book, *The Power of Now,* Eckhart Tolle shares that "Zen masters use the word Satori to describe a flash of insight, a moment of no mind and total presence." He goes on to say that "Although satori is not a lasting transformation, be grateful when it comes, for it gives you a taste of enlightenment."

It happened one evening during my last few days in Schwabisch Hall while I was watching a YouTube video which was pushed to me in my business email. These emails contain options to watch short to long video clips of Deepak Chopra, Wayne Dyer, Eckhart Tolle, and others, sharing their knowledge and wisdom. That particular evening I chose to listen to a clip by Deepak. I would love to be able to share the name of that video, but I have never been able to find it again. After studying with Deepak, immersing myself in his healing programs, reading his books, and teaching his meditation seminar for over two decades, I had heard him speak similar words many times. However, this time, I heard something at a level much deeper than I had heard it before. Deepak said "Your thoughts do not belong to you, and once you understand that, then you can be the author of your destiny." On that night, all cozied up in my bed, with nineteen days of panchakarma treatments under my belt, and likely in response to my many prayers and pleadings for health, well-being, and direction, the words were sent to me again. And I believe they were sent to assist me in healing the trauma of a thirty-year journey of playing the role of wingman to loved ones who struggle with addiction.

A huge part of my life has included up close and personal experiences with addiction, and the ways that addiction can rip the lives of your loved ones right out from under you. I have deeply and dearly loved people who have struggled with addiction. A significant piece of the healing I was trying to accomplish on this sojourn was to metabolize a way to understand, and to heal, the gut-wrenching heartache from watching the ones I love so much, struggle. I didn't know anything about addiction growing up, at least not at a conscious level. But it has been on my plate to understand, and to learn from, since my early twenties. Well, I should reframe that. I think I brought the intention and desire to understand this lesson with me from a prior incarnation. *No joke!* I think some people refer to that as past life merit. The challenge for me right now is to figure out a way to share the moment of instant awakening I experienced that early July night. I think I can best do that by sharing another story. Here's the story.

When I was very young and growing up in Calgary, Alberta, I would hear my grandmother, my mom, and my aunts talk about cancer. The cancer "That runs in our family and that I (we) will likely get." I was young when I started to grasp these messages. I would say that I was four, five, six plus years old. I found their talk perplexing and quite scary. I can remember times in my life hearing one female relative or another say things like "I'm waiting to get my cancer." I did not want to have anything to do with this thinking. I was immersed in a consciousness with these messages of fear, cancer, death, and the ultimate "It runs in our family."

Over the course of my life, two of my maternal aunts did get and die from cancer, as did my maternal grandmother. My mother and my younger sister are cancer survivors. I have watched how this consciousness has played out over several decades. I realized at a young age that I could choose different thoughts then the ones I found myself immersed in. I remember thinking things like "I'm not going to play this game. I'm going to decide not to get cancer. They can't make me think thoughts like they do." Some of my method consisted of an adolescent's approach to scary things, but I also realized at some level as I started to consciously evolve, that we do in fact have the ability to choose our thoughts, and by doing so we have the ability to profoundly affect our physical, mental, and emotional well-being. I again reflected on Deepak's message that "If you want to know what your thoughts have been like up until now, examine your body today; and if you want to know what your body will look like in the years to come, examine your thoughts today."

The person who helped to personalize this message for me was a medical doctor who I met when I first attended Deepak's week-long healing program in 1995. During his wellness consultation with me, I shared with the doctor our family history of cancer, and how I had watched family members expect to get cancer, and wait to get cancer, and how that thinking had scared the bejesus out of me at a very young age. He looked at me and asked me to close my eyes and had me breathe deeply. After several minutes of silence, he led me through a reflective exercise, where he guided me to go back generations and generations and see all of the females in my family as healthy and happy. He then guided me forward to see myself, my children, and all future generations as cancer free and healthy. He said "Centuries ago there was a mistake in consciousness that your family agreed to participate in. Not at a conscious level, but nevertheless, there was an agreement. You can choose to see this as a mistake in consciousness and go on and live a cancer free life, and watch the next generations of your family members do the same thing. It is a choice to belief the family history or not." Those were some of the most affirming words that I had ever heard in my life. They validated what I had believed about how we can choose to think different thoughts. It was spectacular to feel my beliefs so confirmed.

I can also tell you that stepping out of a family consciousness is not without its challenges. My mother has had the BRCA1 gene test done; so has my uncle, my older sister, my younger sister, and her daughter. My mother, in particular, has expressed her shock and disappointment that I am not interested in having the test performed. I have shared with them, that according to my research, that testing positive for the gene test does not mean that I will get cancer, and testing negative does not mean that I will not get cancer. I have also shared that how I care for myself, my preventative practices, and my annual physicals, including Breast MRI's, are good enough for me. I have referred them to articles written by Dr. Bruce Lipton and Dr. Christiane Northrup, who echo my beliefs. In his book, *The Biology of Belief*, Dr. Lipton shares that "It is not gene-directed hormones and neurotransmitters that control our bodies and our minds; our beliefs control our bodies, our minds and thus our lives. . .Oh ye of little belief." Dr. Lipton also states that "While the media made a big hoopla over the discovery of the BRCA1 and BRCA2 breast cancer genes, they failed to emphasize that ninety-five percent of breast cancers are not due to inherited genes."

In her book, *Goddesses Never Age*, Dr. Christiane Northrup shares her perspective on gene testing for breast cancer. She poses the question "Should you test for genes that, if expressed, would cause a serious illness or disease? My feeling is that you should make your decision based on what you plan to do with the information – and ask yourself if it's really information you need." She continues "Fewer than 5 percent of cancers are associated with genetics. Finding out you have, say, the BRCA1 gene mutation associated with breast cancer doesn't mean you will get breast cancer. Finding out you don't have it doesn't mean you won't get it, either. What's more, genetic tests can be very unreliable because they usually sequence only a small sample of your complete genome, so making a decision based on a genetic test is like trying to figure out someone's personality from looking at one snapshot."

For me, I do not care to have the tests performed because I do not want to give my mind the opportunity to run amuck with fears. I don't want to fear my breasts. I prefer to love my breasts and to have a special someone love them too. I focus on living a healthy, dis-ease free life. I also remember Deepak sharing at one of his seminars that he was convinced, after his long career as a medical doctor that more people die from the diagnosis of cancer than ever from cancer itself, because it is what the mind does with the information that can most adversely affect us. I choose to continue to believe in a cancer free life, to focus on how my thinking affects my health and well-being, and to choose my thoughts wisely.

So I see the cancerous thinking in a family as an example of what I heard Deepak say on the YouTube video that evening in Schwabisch Hall. "Your thoughts are not your thoughts" means that our thoughts have been shaped and formed by the collective consciousness, our family consciousness, and a consciousness that was present even in the womb. It is part of the "hypnosis of social conditioning." And until we bring this to a level of awareness we cannot be the author of our own destiny. Got it! But until I reheard the words that night, I had never thought about them in relation to my incomprehensible anguish from watching the people I love so much struggle with addiction. It is such a gut-wrenching journey that has dropped me into the fetal position on my living room carpet on many occasions. But after those weeks of Ayurvedic nourishment, panchakarma, meditation, and deep rest, I *heard* it. What a divine example of how the *Universe* conspires on our behalf to help us along our paths. I had a moment of instant awakening when I realized that the same shift in consciousness I had metabolized in my life regarding cancer, was possible to metabolize in the realm of addiction. I was shown a glimpse of that possibility, and I don't yet have the words to describe how that insight felt inside of me. It was a fleeting moment of the possibility of bliss, of freedom, and of grace, even in the midst of loving someone who struggles. It was omnipotent, omnipresent, and omniscient.

Changing my thinking in the realm of addiction is trickier though, at least it is for me. It requires a more subtle introspection to get a grip on what the existing family consciousness was as I grew up. Let me share some of the challenges, and in doing so deepen my own understanding at a cellular level. And hopefully, offer a contribution to the lives of many of you who may have had similar journeys and heartache. There is so much to be said about the exploration of consciousness and addiction. For now, I will try to wrap glimpses and insights into words.

One of the tough things for me was having had no understanding of addiction prior to my marriage. Or at least I was under that impression. Reflecting back after three decades, I can now see that I was immersed in the consciousness of addiction from a very young age. And I did participate in the thinking and the belief system. The difference is when it was about cancer, I heard talk about it all of the time. I was immersed in the worry, the concern, and the "Oh my God, I'm going to get it I just don't know when." That was my family consciousness. But out there in the world, the message was also everywhere by the time I was a teenager in the mid 70's. There were tests for cancer. Saranwrap was going to give you cancer. My best friend's mother had a double mastectomy and from her hips to her chin she looked like a train had run across her body and gutted her chest cavities. The Surgeon General had mandated that a warning be put on all cigarette packages that smoking can be harmful to your health. I remember the big cancer buzz everywhere. And typically, without questioning, we metabolize the messages and we bring forward family diseases.

So cancer was out loud and everywhere. Addiction has a different energy and it plays a different kind of game. It is illusive and disguised. It is a dis-ease of secrets and lies. It's provocative and charming with its own seductiveness. To be immersed in the "family gathering" consciousness can be fun and entertaining, with music, dancing, and lots of laughter. I have laughed harder and more often with people, who over the course of their lives have developed serious addictions, than with anyone else. I left my first husband after only twenty-one months of marriage because I had learned that he could only laugh with me when he was high. He loved his weed. I wanted to spend my time with someone who could be more present and who could remember the things we talked about and the plans we made. And I wanted a partner who could laugh with me because there are so many absurdly entertaining aspects to life, not because they were high. I just wanted a healthy family. That is all I have ever really, really wanted. And it has eluded me. But now I have caught a glimpse.

I have often wondered why I have had such an attractor magnet to people who struggle with addiction. I have never consciously entered a relationship with someone who struggles with addiction. It is much more an anomaly than that and it is typically hidden. There was a time in my life, during my late twenties, when I sat down and charted how many people in my life were addicted to various substances. At that point, I had about five years of conscious learning about addiction. I was living in it. I was learning. I was new to the journey. So one day I sat down with a piece of poster board and I plotted out how many people in my life struggled with addiction. Actually "struggle" is my word. Most of these people did not appear to be unhappy or struggling. My perception was that they "struggle." On this board I drew a circle with me inside the circle and then arrows pointing out in every direction. The arrows pointed to: a former partner, my current partner, my hair dresser, the woman who did my word processing for me, a family member, three dear friends, two neighbors, a counselor I was referred to when going through a divorce, my office mate on campus, and the list continued. It was very striking to me. Many of these people were referrals to me, not people who I just went out and attracted. It would be decades later while attending a Chopra Center seminar where I listened to Deepak and David banter about addiction and how we humans are by nature, addictive beings. David said that we all have addictive tendencies and that we must be mindful to be addicted to healthy practices. Deepak jokingly responded that he was not addicted to anything and David looked at him, laughed, and said, "Yes you are, you are addicted to thinking."

I have often felt that the gift of addiction has been on my plate, in part, to lead me to a higher state of consciousness, a lesson that I likely did ask for. I do believe that we enter a contract with God or a higher Being before we incarnate. To me, God is the highest possible state of consciousness, not a dead white male. I personally believe that Buddha, Krishna, Jesus, Mother Teresa, Gandhi, Mandela, the Dalai Lama, and others are all examples of people who attained Christ or God Consciousness and that it is possible for each of us to attain.

I do think we ask for the lessons we would like to learn. And I do think that life provides the perfect people, the perfect situations, and the perfect circumstances that allow us an opportunity to metabolize a level of self-awareness that leads us on our path to enlightenment. I suspect I chose *big*! In his book, *Free to Love Free to Heal*, Dr. David Simon shares a giggle, "I have yet to meet a person who remembers choosing to incarnate. Although I can imagine a scenario in which a free floating soul watches a couple having sex and decides, 'I'm going to incarnate into that dysfunctional family.'" I was likely one of those free floating souls.

The thing that I wanted to *know* and to understand when I was a young teenager was, "What is wisdom?" I actually remember feeling a sense of urgency to understand what wisdom was. I was crystal clear that I wanted it. As I entered my twenties, I was consciously asking to know "God's thoughts." I wanted to think

God's thoughts. And what permeated my life? More watching the ones I love struggle with addiction. I can't remember exactly where it was that I first read the Serenity Prayer, but it was during my last year of junior high school. I had seen it framed and hanging in someone's home. The prayer reads "God Grant Me the Serenity to Accept the Things I Cannot Change, Courage to Change Those Things I Can, and the Wisdom to Know the Difference." I had a good sense of what serenity was and a good sense of what courage was, but my, oh my, how I wanted wisdom. Was it a coincidence that I would spend decades being the wingman for people struggling with addiction, and that the Serenity Prayer is the adopted prayer for nearly all rehab programs and AA Meetings?

How, how, how does it all link up? Addiction, wisdom, God's thoughts? One response that I now have is that I am and have always been a seeker. Now hold on to your shorts, I would also pronounce to the world that the people who have graced my life and who struggle with addiction are the ultimate seekers. Yes. That's true. It took me a while to see that with clarity. They are seeking, albeit in the wrong places, but they are seeking. Many people who I have taught Primordial Sound Meditation to have shared with me that some of their experiences with meditation are very much like the "highs" and the "places I access" with drugs. I would argue that they are tapping the same higher consciousness that I tap when I slip into the pure stillness during meditation. The difference is with meditation the experience is healthy and sustained. With drugs and alcohol or whatever the addiction, the experience is not sustained. And instead of complementing our health, it depletes us and moves us away from our natural homeostasis and interrupts our ability to become self-aware.

What the heck does all of this have to do with my story? What aspects of my story came unconsciously filtered from others? What did I hear along my journey? How has this thinking dominated an area of my life and brought me to the brink of broken? I guess my earliest memories are of my paternal great uncle, who allowed us to move into his basement suite when I was four years old when my parents divorced. I loved my uncle. He was happy and funny, and really smart. By the time I was a young teenager I could see that my uncle definitely enjoyed drinking. He continued to be a delight to be around until the stumbling and the passing out took over. I rarely saw him after we left Canada, but when he visited us the pattern was always the same. He eventually died from alcoholism.

I remember my father making beer in the bathtub and having beer and goldfish-swallowing contests with his Air Force buddies. *Fun, fun, fun.* I was a tiny kid then. As I grew up my mom frequently spoke about the alcoholism on my father's side of the family. She said my father drank too much and that my uncles drank too much. She also told me stories of how my paternal grandmother was a pharmacist and had died of an overdose. Except on the rare occasion when I saw my father with his buddies, I never saw any drinking or drug use. My mother remarried a man who became the father who raised me, and I only know of him drinking once. I do, however, remember some of the moms in the neighborhood talking about taking their daily valium.

I was not around or exposed to my paternal side of the family from age eight upwards. Not until I relocated to be with the man on the handsome steed. During my time with this man, I was also in close proximity to the paternal side of my family. Prior to this direct experience with my family members all I knew were the stories I had been told and I wasn't convinced that the stories were true. My mother and father rarely spoke after divorcing, and even today, they are equally happy to never set foot on each other's path. As a result, I added a grain of salt to the stories I would hear about "Your father's side of the family." But after spending the best part of eighteen months getting to know this side of my family, I can tell you that, yes, there is a consciousness of addiction. I learned that one of my uncles was an "Alcoholic who became sober forty years ago." I also observed that my father very conscientiously drinks. I never saw him drink very much and there was definitely a cautious awareness about it. One relative struggles with excessive drinking and two others can keep right up with him. After they spend an evening together drinking, the next morning the three of them combined, will not be able to recall most or any of the prior evening. I also observed the drinking habits of one or two of their children who I would recommend keeping a watchful eye on. Even an adopted family member most definitely has a drinking problem. There is a family consciousness of addiction whether they are aware of it or not.

Heavy drinking was ever present at each of the family gatherings during my time with them. I would also describe their family dynamic as fun! For the most part they are a fun, light-hearted group. They definitely enjoy laughing. But everything also stays at a surface level. Nothing real gets talked about. There was very little real emotion shared. Nobody called anybody out on rudeness or poor behavior. It was like this drunken little party where we keep it fun and keep the broom close to sweep everything under the carpet. There was an underlying feeling of *numb* in the air. It was also a time in my life that I drank more than I ever have. For me, a couple of glasses of wine a couple of times a week is a lot of drinking. Why did I do it? Numbing, that's why. And I suspect unconsciously to "fit in."

I was sad to see and to learn how emotionally unavailable my family members were; and how judgmental and unaccepting some of them were. I desired to get to know them and to be known by them. I had a lifetime of stories to share and I wanted to hear their stories. Most members of this family had met my thirty-eight-year-old daughter once, and only one cousin had ever met my thirty-one-year-old son. I have ached for deeper connections to family my entire life and I was coming to grips with the fact that those connections were not going to be realized with this particular family of people. It was very sad indeed. I found my father to be a very nice and polite man with a great sense of humor; but deep inside of me I ached for a connection that I was coming to realize was not part of the grand plan for this relationship. I consider myself an involved, engaged, devoted, parent and I adore my own children. Somewhere in the recesses of my soul I think I had hoped that my father would feel a similar connection with me. But that was not my experience. I sensed a lack of emotional availability from many of these family members. There was a blessing though. And the blessing was that life provided me another opportunity to see that everybody is doing the best they know how to with their current level of consciousness.

The great news is that when I returned to Seattle, I picked up the phone and called my mother and told her that I was raised by the right parent in the right country. I think that made her life! I don't think she ever thought she would hear those words from me. Nor did I ever think I would speak them.

With some thoughtful analysis, what I am really seeking are the messages and inherent meanings that became part of my Being with reference to addiction, and why I have attracted it into my life. And *why* it has been my toughest lesson. I think that the first insight that I have is the *fun* part. I experienced the fun when I was tiny watching my father and his buddies. The people who I dated and subsequently married were fun, fun, fun. My best friend and I have ached from laughing like no other people I know. Fun has definitely been an attractor magnet. But I seem to be the only one who can have as much fun not drinking, or smoking, or using other substances. I am a whack job with a crazy good sense of humor.

I think I was also protected at a young age from the not so fun part of addiction. I did not see the hangovers or hear any fighting about drinking. Those things definitely existed but they were kept behind closed doors. It is such a silent, sneaky dis-ease. So there's that piece, and there is the embarrassment factor that keeps the offender silent and the enabling factor that silences the protectors. That leaves the potential for a whole lot of confusion and a lot of blanks to be filled in by young unsuspecting minds.

I was also struck by some of the stories that my uncle, who has been sober for forty years, shared with me. Who, by the way, was the only elder in the family who authentically expressed a desire to get to know me and to learn about my life and my children. He spoke about my paternal grandfather and grandmother. I never knew them. I think they died when my father was young. But the story that has survived the generations is that my grandfather was quite an asshole. He cheated and lied and drank. He had a vicious temper and my uncle recalled watching him drag my grandmother by her hair across the kitchen floor.

I think that both the spoken and the unspoken aspects of the consciousness that we are immersed into, the ones that shape and form our thinking and our behaviors, are equally potent. I would also argue that in addition to the silence and the spoken words, there is a memory at a cellular level that gets passed on to future generations. Medical and scientific researchers lean toward looking at our genes. I am suggesting that we look at the cellular memories that get handed down from generation to generation. How do we do that? The same way that lovely doctor did when he took me on a reflective journey back many generations and forward many generations regarding the cancerous family consciousness that has permeated my maternal family. How can we heal those memories? First, we must bring them to a level of our awareness, and then the practice of meditation is the best way I know of to heal and restore balance at those cellular levels.

So how has the history of addiction in my family influenced my life story? I think the piece that has permeated my life was the inability to be fully and lovingly present on the part of the person struggling. And I can't say that I ever really knew or felt that I was loved by these people. That piece has definitely kicked my butt. I think my barometer for measuring what constitutes love, how loving behavior looks and feels, and what it means to have people be fully present and available, was smashed when I was a very young child. The silence of the dis-ease and the absence of "presence" have had tremendous power in shaping my story. And I attracted relationships with men who could not be fully present either due to their addiction or through their physical absence, or both. And the dis-ease of secrets and lies also infiltrated my thoughts. Unless you have experienced it, the deceit feels like a game, and you can't possibly know how disorienting, disconfirming, and disillusioning it feels. I suspect though that many, many of you know exactly what I'm talking about. It is a life of illusion and distortion.

The immersion in the energy of the lies is crazy making. But only when you realize that you are immersed. It is a life of feeling blindsided. What you think is real in your life and in your relationship with the one who struggles, is not real. It becomes the most helpless feeling. Learning how to move forward and let go is tough as nails. The professionals in the field are very heavy handed with their label makers. For the person struggling with addiction, they are labeled an addict, a liar, a thief, a deviant, and they are told that this will always be a monkey on their back; and once an addict, always an addict. For the partner/family member, we are labeled a co-dependent, a rescuer, a doormat, an enabler, and the program professionals are typically secretly searching to see if you are also an addict so they can admit you into the program. All of these ways of speaking and thinking were definitely tossed my way and have had an enormous impact on my story.

If the medical system would view addiction as a dis-ease like they do cancer, then maybe they could find a healing path for those who struggle. When our loved ones are in and out of remission with cancer, we do not call them deviant and get disgusted by them like many people do if our loved ones are in and out of remission with addiction. When will we evolve enough to provide loving, healing environments for the ones we love who struggle with addiction? How do we evolve past the stigma? What is the right message to send to them? For me, love is always the answer. Years ago, during one of his seminars, I remember Wayne Dyer talking about a loved one who had struggled with addiction and how family and friends had all gathered in a circle and expressed to the one struggling, the heartache, the loss, the helplessness, the agony, and the pain that they each felt. Wayne Dyer said that if he would have known then what he now knew that he would have sat in that circle and asked everybody to express only their love, their joy, their happiness, and the blessing that the person who struggled with addiction had brought to their lives.

At a more quantum level, I think that like cancer, addiction gets passed through the generations not by genes but by memories at a cellular level. And in the case of addiction the memories are particularly distorted, so much so that our very cells take on a distorted shape and function. We need to treat that!

Today there are a few addiction treatment programs that I am aware of that offer quality, loving, healing environments. The most comprehensive healing program that I know of is The Chopra Addiction and Wellness Center in Squamish, British Columbia. I highly recommend it.

My thoughts and fears about addiction have been a part of my story for a long time now. What parts of that story serve me at all? What parts do I want to keep? What if I let go of all thinking about addiction? How do I provide love and support to the ones who struggle and not get my life off track and off center? How do I attract a healthy man into my life? What thoughts are preventing that? How do I know for certain that I am worthy of a man being fully present to love me? Self-love and self-awareness are the answers. Meditation is the way. I think at the heart and soul of addiction is the experience of a spiritual disconnect. Meditation is the way to heal the perceived disconnect. There is no real disconnect. We just think that there is and our thinking makes it so.

What shadow aspects of me have I again given voice to from my upbringing that I need to bring to my awareness to heal? What light could I shine on that darkness within me? What is the gift? After many, many, deeply reflective moments, I was starting to see that I had an unconscious distorted perspective on trust as a result of the family consciousness of addiction. I have often experienced an inner conflict in my relationships. My gut has given me cautious, do not trust signals, and I would seek confirmation of truth and honesty through conversations with my relationship partners, who I would allow to convince me of a truth which only strengthened the distortion and weakened my ability to trust my gut. I am starting to see that the lies that have permeated my life in my relationships were not nearly as destructive as the dishonor I did to myself by silencing my own inner guidance. I have unconsciously cast a shadow, a darkness, on my own gut voice. I have silenced my own pure guidance and caused a serious distortion in my own intuitive discernment. I am realizing that I was so focused on the lies and the stories told by others that have blindsided me again and again, and not seen or taken responsibility for, the dishonesty I was responsible for each time I lied to myself by dishonoring my own intuitive spiritual guidance. *Holy crap!* This is huge. This is something I have control over instead of flailing in the world of deceit, lies, and illusion that I have blamed on others. I have been unconsciously sabotaging my own life.

So can you hear dear Reader the power of Deepak's words "Your thoughts do not belong to you, and once you understand that, then you can be the author of your destiny." What family consciousness were you born into? What illnesses run in your family? How has your core belief system affected your well-being and the story that you live out loud? What facets of your story have attracted health and wellness? Which ones have not? How might *you* move beyond your story?

I cannot leave this section on addiction without honoring these people that I have attracted into my life and without looking at the gifts that these relationships have brought to my life. These profound and beautiful relationships were the impetus for my decades of research into healing traditions, modalities, and ultimately consciousness itself. I may not have discovered Ayurveda without you. I would not be the consciously evolving person that I am, without you. I may not have adopted the practice of meditation into my life, without you. I may not have laughed as hard as I have laughed, without you. I may not have been dropped to the depths of sorrow that I have known, without you. Without the sorrow I may not have developed the depths of empathy and compassion that guide my life. I may have never discovered my innate ability to be healthy, grounded, and move away from judgement, without you. I may have never learned to honor and feel the wealth of human emotions that I allow myself to feel, without you. Your presence in my life has called me to question my core beliefs about God, disease, meditation, healing, spirituality, and being human. And the path of that questioning has served my conscious evolution. You have gifted me with my greatest lessons and played the role of great teachers. *Thank you. From the core of my Being, thank you!*

Don't separate yourself spiritually from anyone
regardless of where they might live or how
different their appearances or customs may be
from your own.

Wayne Dyer

Chapter Eight

New Friends, Healing Waters, and a Cemetery

I was really enjoying Marienbad. It was the perfect size, extremely walkable, outrageously beautiful, and the architecture was remarkable. It is a magical combination of parks, noble homes, and pavilions and colonnades which house or protect the hundred natural mineral springs. It was now week two and I was feeling a bit more energized. I had my daily routine down. It had remained the same as the first week. Each day began with going to the tiny gym, and then eating breakfast followed by aquafit, long walks, and added pool time between lunch and dinner. Since the regular aquafit class continued to be about eighteen minutes in length, I had learned to pilfer some of the workout equipment and set it aside for my own workout later each day. Hans, the German man who continued to be so helpful showing me what my feet should be doing underwater during class, was an absolute delight. It seemed his English was getting better every day. I was grateful since I was still bumbling around with German. He shared with me that his wife didn't like the music he listens to and asked me to join the two of them on the outside deck for Social Hour. I did join them, and within minutes he and I both had a set of headphones plugged into his i-Pad and we were listening to Cold Play. I was delightfully surprised with his music selection and thoroughly enjoyed hearing songs in English, words I actually understood and could sing along with. I had been immersed in foreign languages for over a month now. And I continued to love that. I still couldn't understand anyone's stories and I couldn't go on and on about my own. It provided me with such a marvelous amount of time to continue to examine my story and how it was, or was not, serving my health and well-being.

I had my eating routine down to a science. Much of the food was actually pretty tasty. But during my second week the whole buffet thing was starting to get to me a bit. They had beautiful fish, meats, cheeses, scrumptious breads, and once a week a flowing fountain of chocolate for pineapple dipping. *Clever.* Since I am not a meat, cheese, bread, or chocolate girl, I gravitated toward the fish and the salad bar. I had learned that in Czechia there is a lot of pickled food. I was hopeful that it would be possible for me to handle about one more week of all of the pickled stuff. There was pickled herring, pickled carrots, pickled radishes, pickled pickles, pickled beets, pickled onions, pickled cauliflower, pickled salmon, and I suspect that some of the desserts that I didn't eat were pickled too. I sat alone by an open window for every breakfast and tried to do the same for lunch. I had met some interesting women at our small assigned seating dinner table. It appeared that they seat "solo" female travelers near the back of the room with other "solo" female travelers. The vast majority of people staying at this resort were married couples about the age of my parents, and blended into the crowd were a few families with school-aged children.

During the entire second week my dining partners were the same two women. One woman, Emma, spoke no English and the other woman, whose name completely eludes me, spoke a little English and would play the role of translator. They were both German. Emma and I frequented the lounge after dinner for drinks, or no drinks, and to enjoy live music. We laughed a lot and even danced together on a few occasions but rarely understood a word that we spoke to one another. Laughter and dancing worked. We enjoyed Czech Elvis impersonators, female opera singers, and even a lecture or two in the evenings. I attended the first lecture hoping that the slides that were shown would provide me with a clue as to what was being shared. Nope. I didn't understand a single thing, except the word Hitler, which was spoken several times.

I liked Emma. I had learned through our translated conversations that she spent three months on a cruise ship and that the cost was 30,000 euro. Somewhere in the story a man figured into the equation, but I believe he turned out to be somewhat of a deadbeat and that she may have tossed him overboard at one of the first ports of call. She was planning another several-month cruise that would take her to the whole of South America. *I think.* I really liked the other woman too, but I had yet to understand her name. A very unusual name pronounced with a very strong German accent. One evening she shared with me that there was some kind of day-long tour scheduled for the next morning and that I should go to the front reception desk and get the information, which I did. I understood that the bus would be leaving at 10:00 a.m. the next morning and that the cost was eleven euros. We would return at 18:00 hours. I signed up, paid my eleven euros, and had absolutely no idea where I would be going. I was happy to see my nameless friend on the bus in the morning.

It was a long bus ride, almost two hours. The tour was hosted by this delightful Czech gentleman. He narrated the entire two hours. I understood words like Hitler, war, and that's about it. The scenery was beautiful. There were windy roads, old-stone-moss-covered bridges, and thick forested areas. We passed through several little villages with an occasional siting of small castles tucked away in the greenery before arriving in Karlovy Vary, as the Czech people call it. The German people call it Carlsbad. I had noticed that there was typically a little tension in the air between the German people, the Czech people, and the Russian people. My ear had not developed well enough yet to discern which language the people were speaking. But hints of animosity were clearly present.

Karlovy Vary was a much larger city than Marienbad. Both were "spa healing" cities but in Karlovy Vary there were many, many more free flowing fountains with healing waters. It was quite amazing to see people lined-up waiting for their turn to fill their hands or containers with water from the fountains. Small children would fill empty plastic bottles, drink it all, and get right back in the lines. I tasted the water twice. Once at a free flowing fountain near a stream in the woods in Marienbad. I was on a guided Nordic walk with the young man leading the walk and two other women. He encouraged us to try the water but also warned not to drink too much because some people have trouble making it back to the bathroom in time. Thank goodness someone was able to share that little tidbit in English with me. The water contains a very high sulfur content and has a strong salty taste. I'm forever grateful that I only had a few sips because even then the nearest bathroom seemed very far away. The water is curative and has a strong laxative effect. On a side note, one of the primary reasons that I chose to stay at the Velkolepý, was because they had an active fitness program which included aquafit and Nordic walking daily. I wanted to do both every single day. And both were on the schedule every day, but in the entire twenty-one days, we only went Nordic walking once. I was informed by the young man leading the walk that "Russian people not so much for this, so we not do."

Karlovy Vary had very similar architecture to Marienbad, although older and was much bigger and more bustling with people. The natural curative fountains were everywhere and were contained in even more grand pavilions and colonnades. Karlovy Vary also attracted more tourists than Marienbad. I was glad that I experienced it but also very happy that I chose the smaller scale Marienbad as the place to spend my twenty-one days. We completed our day with a tour of the infamous Grandhotel Pupp (pronounced Poop) which is the hotel in the movie *The Last Holiday* starring Queen Latifah. It was fun to experience and looked just like it did in the movie. As we departed Karlovy Vary we also drove past the high dam where they shot the bungie jumping scenes in the movie. My new, nameless friend asked me to send her all of the photos that I took of the Grandhotel Pupp. I was happy to oblige and I asked her for her contact information. I'm still looking for that scrap of paper, which by the way did not include her name. Dammit.

I was enjoying the culture of the Czech people. When I first arrived I found a high level of "couldn't-care-less" impersonal type of communication. I figured it was a cultural phenomenon and that maybe many of the people just didn't like English speakers. As the days passed, I found a deepening abruptness and rudeness. My first thought was "Holy cow what a great place for me to come and teach interpersonal communication seminars." Within a few more days I realized that they do not care a bean about being more interpersonal. Hans said that it was "Customary treatment from the Czech people and that it is remnant behavior from communism." He had a long career as a consultant and said that he was going to speak with management. I was starting to find some of what I had initially thought of as abrasive, as entertaining. It was a different type of curtness than what I have experienced in North American cultures. Czech people just didn't care and didn't have the time of day. Behind most interactions was what felt like, get out of my way and why are you here? But they were not mean. If you have thin skin you might not like the experience. I was becoming more and more fascinated with the dynamic and it only contributed to exercising my smile muscles.

Mid-week, my new, dear, nameless friend invited me to drive with her to a castle town about an hour's drive away. She had driven to Marienbad from her home in Germany and had her car at the ready. I was delighted to join her. I spent time during our ride asking her how to say things in German. Like her name! The drive took us back the same route that we had taken on our tour day to Karlovy Vary, until we veered off on another country road. We arrived at the castle town of Bečov nad Teplou or Petschau as the German people say. It was an enchanting, ancient, little village with a street fair in progress. There was music and children dancing in the streets, and booths set up with local artists presenting their lovely creations. I saw something I have never seen at a street fair. There were yoga balls in round holders on the ground and little children were beating the heck out of them with drumsticks. I went straight for the food. I walked past the pickled, pickled, pickled tables until I came upon the sausage, brat, and beer table. I ordered a bavorska klobasa for 65 czk and a cold beer. Yes, indeed. I enjoyed that meal so much. I ate at a picnic table that was as old as the hills and looked over the valley. Ancient everywhere! *God I love ancient.* My soul adores being steeped in history. I walked down the streets and ran my fingertips along the old stone walls and I felt the whispers of times gone by. And I wondered, "Have I been here before." Feelings of familiarity surged through my Being.

I bought handmade herb soaps from a young lady outside of the castle. She grew the herbs and made the soaps. The air smelled of a sweet, lavender-sage mix. *Yum.* And the vendor tables nearest the castle where lined with homemade cheeses. I have always wanted to bring home with me the smells of foreign lands; well most of them, some of the cheeses smelled a bit repugnant. We toured the castle. It was a guided tour which did me a heck of a lot of good since the guide was speaking Czech. There was lots of old stuff and a story that went with it. There were, however, some descriptive note cards written in English. Those cards described the metal and woodworking artists' tools. Wouldn't you know it, the only items that I recognized and was familiar with, were the ones with the cards written in English.

We returned to Marienbad in time for dinner. Saturday dinner nights were special with a predetermined menu served as several courses and presented to us at our table. Everything was beautifully plated. My new, dear friend was leaving the following day to return to her home in Germany. She was going to stop along the way and spend the night in a charming bed and breakfast. I asked Emma what my dear friend's name was. Emma didn't appear to understand my question, but then she spoke a word that sounded like the right name. *Bla soo pal a ba?* I give up. Emma and I went to listen to music upstairs after dinner. She would be leaving in two more days and I would be leaving in five. I couldn't believe that my twenty-one days in Marienbad was almost over. I had been trying to find the most cost effective travel from Marienbad to Prague, the nearest major airport. Of course trains are the cheapest but I didn't know if I had the three train rides followed by a shuttle travel day in me, with my still heavy case and backpack. I inquired about cost-effective travel at tourist information kiosks. One woman spoke enough English to tell me about a shuttle that would pick me up at my hotel and take me directly to the Prague airport. It would cost the equivalent of 125 euro. Much more than I wanted to spend but she also told me that if I could find people leaving the hotel on the same day, that cost would be divided. So I was on a mission, saying to everyone I encountered at the hotel, "Hallo, you going bye-bye in two days?"

My last few days in Marienbad continued to be very reflective days. A gentleman, who had noticed that I took long walks every day, approached me in the hotel lobby and pantomimed for me that across the street and up some stairs there was a path in the woods that led to a cemetery. I was deeply grateful that this man took the time to share with me. I love cemeteries. I do some of my best thinking there and experience some of my deepest moments of gratitude. And dead people are often my favorites. They have this uncanny ability to listen. So I set off across the street, up the stairs, to the path that would lead me there. Once in the woods there were so many paths and I could see the possibility of spending many hours wandering aimlessly and getting very lost. I had been in Marienbad long enough to feel fairly safe venturing into the woods on my own. I started down several different paths that just didn't feel right so I back-tracked to the stairs and reflected on the pantomimed message. I think he had pointed to the right from the top of the stairs. Off to the right I went. The path beckoned me.

The forest there was beautiful. In Germany and Czechia they appear to do a much more brilliant job of deforestation and preservation than in the Pacific Northwest. They don't do the same kind of massacre of forest lands like I have seen in the greater Seattle area and beyond. Instead, they mindfully take some of the trees leaving room for the others to grow into themselves. It was outrageously beautiful. There was enough space between the trees for the light to do its magic. It was absolutely breathtaking. I paused to sit on a simple bench near the foot of a very large fir tree. The light was shining through the trees, hitting the tops of the nearby plants and making them look like jewels on the forest floor. And beyond the trees the light manifested itself in sage and emerald colors in a little meadow. I continued to walk and take it all in. I was immersed in a matrix of greens and streaming light. Hunter green, emerald green, lime green, olive green, all of which assaulted the senses. In areas where the trees were young ones, they appeared to be dancing in strobes of light.

As the trail came to an end, I was standing right in front of the huge wrought iron gate entrance to the cemetery. I was extremely delighted to see a little WC sign fastened to the gate. I assumed that it was not for the residents. Maybe it was a solution to back-of-gravestone urination? *God I love cemeteries.* This one was crowded and as old as time. I adore sitting with ancient and I adore sitting with spirits. I tried to be as still as I could to hear any whispers, and always asked permission to photograph their dwellings. I was so grateful that I came. I wandered through the cemetery, which must have covered acres and acres of land. There were areas that were centuries-old, and new areas. There were potted plants placed on top of graves everywhere, hundreds and hundreds of them, unlike the bouquets of flowers typically seen in cemeteries at home. After about an hour, I came upon an arch with ivy growing up the sides. It was an entrance to the area of the cemetery which honors the Czech (and possibly German) soldiers who fought in both world wars. Rows and rows and rows of concrete cross headstones, often with names filling both sides. As I passed through the arch I discovered a round monument listing the names of, who I understood to be, the commanders.

There was a separate monument commemorating soldiers who fought in World War II. It read "ORIENTIERUNGSPLAN KRIEGSGRABERSTATTE MARIENBAD 1939 – 1945." Which translated into German, means "Orientation Plan War Treasures." Below the German words was the same saying written in Czech. At the base of the monument was a very large notebook made up of metal pages that could be turned, each one containing thousands of names. They were listed last name, first name, date of birth, and date of death. Bretschneider, Bruha, Dittrich, Duman, Ebermaier . . . . . As with all military cemeteries, the uniformity, the straight lines, and rows brought tears to my eyes. I lingered. At the front of this area of the cemetery was a statue of a young sad woman, representing a mother, a wife, a daughter? Maybe she was Mary? At her feet on the ground was a heart made out of tea-light candles and inside the heart were drying irises and what looked like baby's breath. The candles had all burned out. I stayed for quite a while with tears streaming down my cheeks. I wandered back to the front gate of the cemetery and again was surrounded by potted plants on top of the ancient, often moss-covered, graves. There was an occasional empty plastic water jug or pail hanging on a thick metal post with a faucet to water the potted plants. As I reached the front entrance a statue of a sitting angel looking up to the sky with her hands broken off caught my attention. I took several photographs of her. While looking through the lens of my camera I felt a special affinity with that angel. Both of us spending so much time sitting in prayer, looking up for guidance, and a little bit broken. I really wanted to bring her home with me but thought better of that.

I was down to my last two days in Marienbad and was feeling such gratitude that I had made the choice to come here. And I was so glad that I had chosen to stay twenty-one days in each of the two places I had been so far, Schwabisch Hall and Marienbad. It is such a tremendous way to travel. I had also discovered that it is a perfect amount of time. I was ready to leave Schwabisch Hall and I was ready to leave Marienbad. Each had brought such healing, nourishment (except for the pickled stuff), and a gorgeous amount of time for introspection. I caught myself feeling both excitement and hesitation about the next couple of weeks of my journey. My friend, Adara, from home was scheduled to meet me on July 26, in Amsterdam where we had pre-booked Airbnb's for five days and then we would travel to Prague where we would spend six days. At the beginning of my trip when I booked the front and back ends with six unplanned weeks in the middle, I had thought I would not only really want to, but would also enjoy, hooking up with a couple of different friends. Now, I found myself feeling very selfishly ambivalent about sharing my time for the next two weeks. Not a feeling that I anticipated having at all! I had been thoroughly enjoying my self-reflective, healing, *awarefulness* journey. And I was getting a little anxious about how it would feel to transition to typical vacation, tourist stuff for the next two weeks. Overall, I suspected I would be grateful to see a friend. At the moment, however, I was most grateful that I would have five weeks of my sojourn remaining after Amsterdam and Prague. I did not want to give up this time for deep introspection. I did not want to give up being immersed in foreign languages. I did not want to give up all of the stillness and quiet.

Hallelujah! I found out that two other people would be heading to the Prague airport on the same shuttle that I was taking. That cut the cost tremendously. I was the only person picked up at the Velkolepý, and then we stopped and picked up a man and a woman at another hotel on the main square. The vehicle was not a shuttle bus as I had imagined. It was a small, older, nondescript private car. It was about one hundred and sixty-five kilometers from my hotel to the Prague International Airport. No one else in the car, not the driver, or the couple, spoke a word of English. *Gotta love it.* I sat in the back seat with the husband and his wife sat in the front seat with the driver. She was a chatty Cathy and I was again so grateful that I didn't understand a word. I think the husband wanted to talk as much to me but when he learned that I spoke English he didn't keep trying to engage. I am not sure what she was going on and on about but in the rearview mirror I could see the driver rolling his eyes about every ten kilometers. It appeared that she believed that she was the better driver of the two of them. Aren't I the lucky girl? I typically love engaging with people of other cultures and languages but my gut told me to look out the window and to fake sleeping. After about an hour into the drive to Prague, the driver pulled into the back parking lot of a convenience store. I asked "WC?" and he nodded yes. I got out of the car to use the facilities. As we rounded the corner of the little store and were out of eye-shot of the other passengers, the driver looked at me, put fingers in both ears, rolled his eyes, and shook his head. I gave him a sympathy hug and we shared a great laugh.

A person's judgement says nothing about the person they are judging, it speaks only to their own need to judge.

Wayne Dyer

Chapter Nine

Follow the Leader

I arrived at Vaclav Havel Airport Prague very early and had about four hours to entertain myself before my flight to Amsterdam. I typically never baulk at long airport waits in other countries. I find it absolutely fascinating to watch the mix of people and to suck up the sounds of the foreign languages. I cozied up in a little airport café, plugged in my laptop, and ordered something not pickled to eat. It would be a perfect time to catch up on emails and learn how to upload some of my travel photos onto my Facebook page, which I had never really actively used. Just as I was sinking into my little place of bliss I heard a group of loud Americans chattering, and *pop*, there went my bliss bubble. It was a group of women who had just wrapped up at a conference in Prague. I started to pack up my belongings and go find another spot so I could remain in my faraway, precious place when I heard more American accents from the other direction. I was terribly bummed and I must say that I was also very shocked how much it affected me. I wanted to burst into tears. I had been so far away and immersed in such foreignness for a month and a half and all of the sudden I was surrounded by Americans. It felt like such a violation. Tears started to pour down my cheeks. Nobody was more shocked by my reaction than me. What the heck was that all about? Why such a strong reaction? Maybe it was a little preparation for me to spend the next twelve days with my friend speaking English every day. And of course I was heading to Amsterdam where I would be immersed with English speakers, albeit with accents.

My flight to Amsterdam was on-time and a breeze, but a bit of the Prague airport sadness lingered. I had booked a room for one night at the CitizenM Hotel about one hundred and twenty-five meters from the airport where I would spend the night and meet Adara when she arrived early the next morning. It was a great decision to stay at the CitizenM Hotel. It was very futuristic and felt like the world as it was portrayed in the Jetsons cartoons of the mid 1980's. My room was extremely modern and very high tech. The wall mounted television screen said "Welcome Citizen Cait." Everything was controlled from an i-Pad. The cylinder-shaped shower looked like you could just step into it and be beamed up. It was smart, slick, and innovative. But what won my heart was the sign at the front check-in desk that read, "If we are not here we have just stepped out for lunch, if we are not here in five minutes, we are enjoying dinner too." I laughed out loud and checked in at one of the kiosks. It was simple indeed.

Adara arrived right on time the next morning. I was starting to feel a little grateful for my shocking re-immersion into English the day before at the Prague airport. I was excited to see my friend but I also felt a bit protective of my introspective, soulful journey. I realized that I should just shift gears and jump into the tourist experience and then regroup after our time together. I found the door that Adara would be exiting from and enjoyed a quiet cup of tea. Fifteen minutes later I spotted her exiting through the International Arrivals door.

After quick hugs and good-to-see-ya's, Adara, being the very proud person that she is, announced that she had found the bus that will get us within a couple of blocks of our Airbnb. I was a little ambivalent only because I am crucially aware of taking care of my back on travel days and I was all decked out with my backpack and toting my case. Me, given my heavy case and love for my healthy back, I'd rather err in the direction of paying the extra ten euros and take an Uber, but not Adara. Nope, she got off the plane with just one bag that looked like Mary Poppins' carpetbag. It was sweet but I suspected that the "no wheels" feature might kick her butt a bit by the end of her stay. After inquiring about where to catch the bus, and the right bus, we were in line to board. It was a quick ride to our stop, maybe twenty minutes. Adara had "perfect directions" and off we went. In the wrong direction, three maybe four times, before we found a person who pointed us in the right direction. My body was feeling the discomfort of pulling my case for what felt like miles on the cobblestone streets. Eventually we found our way and checked into our gorgeous little Airbnb. When booking it we had read that our accommodations were on the second floor and that there were no elevators. Yes, second floor but with four narrow and steep flights of stairs, each with at least twenty steps. I had visions of leaving my case on the first level and coming down each day to gather what I needed, but was quickly informed that was not allowed.

Our Airbnb was perfectly located just blocks from the Museum District and had the most amazing patio. It was huge with gorgeous sitting areas overlooking a well-manicured lawn. We loved it. We were literally two blocks from the Rijksmuseum, the Van Gogh Museum, and the Stedelijk Museum. Adara and I set out to find an outdoor market and to enjoy a bite to eat. Within fifteen minutes we were strolling through an amazing market with all of the fresh vegetables, fruit, meats, and flowers that you could imagine. Not a pickled thing in sight. And marijuana products were abundant. I bought a sucker and ate it. The sucker was not too fascinating and my face broke-out the next day. I felt like an eighteen-year-old all over again. But when in Amsterdam!

Late that afternoon we found a patio, enjoyed a cold drink, and watched the passersby. We were sitting outside on a busy street corner where there were lots of pedestrians, bikes, bikes, and more bikes all synchronized in this amazing symphony with the vehicles.

I watched several people park these tiny cars on sidewalks. These little cars, with the word Mango on the front, also looked like they were something out of the Jetson's cartoon. They were about the size of a carry-on! Eventually, a mother and her three young children approached one of the tiny cars. I thought that there was no way possible they were all going to fit inside. But much to my surprise they did! Mom and one small child in the front seats and two smaller children sat on little wooden stools in the back, *simply amazing*. I couldn't get over the small cars and the apparent ability to just pull up on the sidewalk and park. It was truly fun stuff.

We spent the next several days walking everywhere with Adara leading the way. She was intent on finding this old square that I can't for the life of me remember the name of. We walked, walked, walked, and walked, and eventually even asked a couple of credible sources for assistance, like the local police, who pointed us in yet again another direction. We walked well over twelve miles that day in search of the old square. We never found it, at least not that day. But we did find thousands and thousands of bikes and riders navigating right of ways with cars and pedestrians. I knew that Amsterdam was a city of bikes but to experience it was just over the top. It was absolutely fabulous. We had quickly realized that we needed to develop some serious skills to maneuver among them.

During the first few evenings before falling asleep I found myself reflecting deeply on my friendships, especially my female friendships. I hadn't anticipated that I would have an opportunity to continue to examine my story during my time with Adara. One of the qualities that my female friends seem to share is their very strong personalities. I love people, men and women, who have a beautiful sense of themselves. And I don't mind a strong personality. But what I had begun to examine over the last several years in my friendships was the fact that these friends also seemed extremely judgmental. That is a quality that I don't favor in myself or others. What is it that makes some people so judgmental? I find that I do not have a need to judge others because I have honed the ability to see aspects of myself in most everybody, including the good, the bad, and the ugly aspects. And maybe it's also attributable to the fact that I have had my butt kicked over the decades. It seems that anytime I have ever judged others it comes right back to bite me, whether or not I expressed these judgments. There's that frequency thing again. The frequency of the thoughts we choose to have carries a resonance that affects the quality of our relationships, our stories, and of our lives.

I admired that my chosen female friends had a voice and would speak up because I never grew up having a voice. But I did not admire their need to judge and most often to judge harshly. I grew up being silenced if I tried to express my thoughts or opinions. I was raised in an environment that I would describe as dramatic and which lacked boundaries and honoring of one another. I reflected on my relationship with my best friend of thirty-eight years. When we first met she lived in a home that ran a daycare business and when I would drop off my daughter each morning she would riddle me comments such as, "Look at how you have dressed her," "I can't believe that you brought this cereal again," or "I should help you with your make-up, you'd look so much better," or "You need to do something about that hair on your upper lip." I often left that doorstep, walked the twelve paces to my car, and was exhausted from our early morning exchange. But I truly loved and admired her ability to have a voice.

In the two years that I've known Adara I have enjoyed our friendship but this was my first experience ever traveling with her. I realized on day one that she definitely needed to be in control of our plans, our form of travel, etcetera. I was just fine with that in this instance because I knew that after our time together I had another five weeks to go wherever my heart took me and to continue my soul journey. I was struck by how keenly aware I was of her need to call all of the shots. In the evenings I reflected on the friendships I have had over the past several decades, and I would say that I saw a similar pattern. Over the years as I have consciously evolved, I have often cleaned out my friendship networks. I have one dear friend who is still very judgmental and even though I have observed that she has learned to verbally express her judgments far less, she has not healed her need to have judgmental thoughts. So the feeling in the room remains the same whether she spoke her judgments out loud or whether she just thought judgmental thoughts about others. As I ponder the question "What makes a person so judgmental?" I hear Wayne Dyer's words, "A person's judgment says nothing about the person they are judging, it speaks only to that person's need to judge." Why though do we want to judge others? Where does that come from? I guess one response is that it comes from a deep insecurity in the person that feels the need to judge. I suspect that they are also very silently critical of themselves. On the deepest level however, I believe being judgmental reflects an unexamined aspect of our shadow self. It seems to me to be a very hard way to live. Why would people choose to always be comparing themselves to others? How different would our relationships be if we experienced each other as part of the same larger consciousness? Why do some people appear to embrace such entitlement behaviors? As I pondered these questions I drifted off into a deep sleep.

Our days in Amsterdam were filled with strolls down cobblestone streets that meandered over and around the canals of the city. To me, there is an advanced consciousness in Amsterdam. Most people were walking and/or on bikes. It is a very healthy, active, and dynamic city. The culture is open and friendly. The banks carry no cash. The storefronts and window designs are just outstanding, very contemporary, and delightfully creative. Flowers, cheeses, pastries, beer, fresh fruits and vegetables, and cannabis products are everywhere. I stuck with delicious bowls of mussels and their magnificent fresh vegetables.

We visited several museums. Over the years of my travels I have toured some of the greatest museums in the whole of Europe and I'm not a fan of filling a lot of time seeing more. But Adara had pre-purchased tickets and I must admit that I loved touring the Van Gogh Museum. It was beautifully designed and displayed most of Van Gogh's greatest art, with in-depth audios of this man's tortured but genius life. There were open, high-ceiling areas where images of his art were projected on walls and in constant motion. It was quite breathtaking. I was taking photos with my iPhone because I saw other people taking photos. I was quickly told by museum security that that was not allowed. I was quite surprised that they did not make me delete the photos that I took. *Want to see them?*

On another day we toured the red light district. I was taken aback by the ladies in the windows who were clad in next to nothing and playing the role of temptresses. The district was full of "sex palaces" and "erotica outlets." And of course Café Remember. My favorite was probably "Live porno show – Hospital Bar." I guess that one is for people who have an erection lasting longer than four hours.

During one of our last days in Amsterdam while enjoying a stroll through the shops, Adara told me that we would be taking an Uber to a destination outside of the city. She said that she had looked for bus routes but couldn't find one that would get us to our destination. I queried her, but she was tight lipped about where we were going. We enjoyed a late afternoon meal and then changed clothes to go wherever it was we were going. She told me to wear the polka-dot dress that I had bought in Schwabisch Hall and a denim jacket. I obliged. The Uber ride was long indeed. We were miles outside of the city, which was pretty cool to experience. Eventually we arrived at a huge stadium. We hopped out and Adara led the way to the stadium entrance. I saw a variety of bulletin boards displaying different events but I still had no idea what we were going to see and experience, until we got to the ticket collectors and Adara handed them two tickets to see U2's Joshua Tree Concert. I was blown away and extremely excited. The concert was fabulous and we had a grand time. During the concert I kept looking at Adara and chanting *"We are in Amsterdam at a U2 Concert! Can you freaking believe it?"* The whole evening was an outstanding memory in the making.

Getting home from the concert was a bit more of a challenge. Feeling like we sort of knew our way around the city we decided to take the train back. There were several thousand people doing the same thing. Over the loudspeaker, the stadium official announced that there was a problem with one of the regularly scheduled late night trains and stadium personnel were directing us to various platforms with trains heading to a variety of destinations. We got really lucky! There were only a handful of people getting on our train. After boarding and the train left the station we quickly learned that we were heading in the wrong direction. There were two couples from Ireland that had made the same mistake. We all got off at the next stop and hoped and prayed that there were still trains running after midnight to get us back to the city. The couples from Ireland were light-hearted and we all had a good laugh. After two trains, one bus, and a long walk, we eventually found our way home at 3:30 a.m. Needless to say we slept in late that morning.

We continued to explore the city, enjoy wonderful food, and finally on our last day I convinced Adara to go for a boat ride on the canals. She baulked a bit and muttered something about the ridiculousness of my suggestion, but we boarded the boat. There were many tour boat options to choose from. We chose an open-air boat with round tables and chairs with seating for twenty-five. A bar menu was available during our ninety-minute ride. We ate fresh chips and sipped a glass of wine. It was an exceptional way to experience Amsterdam. The brick-lined canals have a life of their own. All imaginable small boats, canoes, kayaks, and live-aboard vessels, line each side of the canals. The captains of the vessels maneuvered with the same type of grace as the cyclists on the streets above. To me, one of the greatest ways to see a city is by boat. It was fabulous. I loved being on the water and could have stayed all day. The captain and servers on our boat had to duck every time we went under a bridge, which was about every fifty yards. Three hours after our tour, I was very surprised when Adara admitted that she had actually really enjoyed the experience.

I loved the narrow, cobblestone streets and the canals of Amsterdam. I loved the people, the markets, and the health of it all. I found myself extremely attracted to their free-thinking, advanced consciousness.

You can be right or you can be happy. The
choice is yours.

Wayne Dyer

Chapter Ten

Armed Guards, Synagogues, and a Political Satirist

We traveled to Prague on July 31. Initially, Adara was insisting on taking a bus to the train station, but with some coaxing she agreed to take an Uber. I think realizing the weight of her own case, the one with no wheels, helped to sway her decision. Plus we had to be at the station by 5:30 a.m. and there were few buses running at that time of day. Adara had taken the liberty of booking our train travel prior to her arrival in Amsterdam. We had a two-train journey to Prague. The first train was fairly easy with plenty of seating available. However, feeling the need for a break and some alone time, I left the car seating area and found my way to the dining car. There was a man working behind the food counter who I can only describe as the "Soup Nazi." Not a friendly fella and there were moments when I suspected that my very smiling presence there was going to get me tossed from the train. It gave me hours of enjoyment watching his interaction with unsuspecting customers. The service resembled something like "You want to eat, you die." Rest assured that I was only laughing on the inside.

The second train was a little more trying. It was an absolutely full train and we were jam-packed into a reserved seating car with very little wiggle room. Again, I chose to leave for the dining car, which was spectacular and only had three other people present and at least nine open tables. It was glorious. Adara refused to leave the cramped car. I have no idea why the majority of the people stay crammed in their seats. I ordered a glass of wine and nuts with raisins. The scenery along the way was beautiful. There were endless gorgeous green fields, meadows with old-stone walls, and forested hillsides. I stayed in the dining car until five minutes before our arrival in Prague when I had to go and collect my case.

Upon our arrival in Prague, Adara did not even hesitate to agree to flag down a taxi with me. What a blessing for my back. I think she was feeling the pain of toting a heavy case and the pain of having been crammed in a crowded seat compartment. We took a taxi to our Airbnb. We couldn't have picked better places to stay in either Amsterdam or Prague. We were literally staying on the main street two blocks down from the Old Town Square, the city's twelfth-century medieval core. The architecture in Prague was an amazing blend of Gothic, Baroque, Romanesque, and Renaissance to name a few. Our accommodations were perfect. Both Amsterdam and Prague Airbnb's had one bedroom, or one bed, so I couched it for the twelve days. Ours was a sweet place which I am thrilled to share, had an elevator! The view out of our window was spectacular. The tiled roof tops were amazing. Old stone buildings, some cream color, others shades of yellow and orange, with Gothic steeples and Romanesque turrets. I could lean out the window and look to the right and see the Old Town Square. It was absolutely thrilling. The sound of hoof beats drew me back to the window and through the trees below I caught sight of horse-drawn carriages.

I had wanted to travel to Prague for well over a decade but hadn't fit it into my previous trips. I couldn't wait to get out and explore. Except for my travel buddy, I was once again immersed in a non-English speaking culture. *Woot! Woot!* We went down our tiny (and I mean tiny) elevator, exited the building, and walked to the right to the Old Town Square. I was stunned and shocked by the extremely high-end shops that lined each side of the street on the way to the square. I was even more shocked that there were large men sporting secret-service type earbuds and armed with guns in each of the shops. They appeared to be in contact with other armed, *earbudded,* men on the street. I have certainly been in areas of the United States, Canada, and Europe where there are very high-end stores and I have shopped in them, or at the extremely high-end I have pretended to shop in them, but I have never witnessed this type of security.

When I travel, I only research my chosen destinations just enough to get myself there safely and to stay in safe places. I do not get guide-books and seek to know everything about an area. I don't do that so I can experience the surprise, and in this instance the shock, of a new city, town, or village. I had imagined a very different Prague before I arrived. I imagined the cobblestone streets and the variety of architecture, but never the armed guards in stores nor the brands that they were protecting. During our entire six days in Prague I rarely saw even one shopper in the stores. I started to suspect that these stores were a front for other Eastern European mafia-type activity; or possibly a headquarters for altering votes that could affect a presidential election. I am fairly certain that I'm right about this.

The Old Town Square was full of people from all over the world. Accents and foreignness, eating and drinking, street performers, huge yellow snakes slithering out of styrofoam coolers, restaurants with outdoor patios, meat cooking on spits, and the worst corn-on-the-cob I have ever tasted. I was taken aback when my attention was drawn to a window with women who were sitting in a pedicure establishment. They were sitting in a row of chairs facing the window with their feet soaking in this long, rectangular pool of water. There were little fish nibbling away at the skin on their feet. I think I threw-up a little bit in my mouth.

The Square itself was very magical. Not quaint like I had imagined but nevertheless magical. The fragrance in the air from the waist-up consisted of the aromas of fresh-baked bread and pizza, barbequed meat, pasta with gorgeous sauces, and ice-cream and gelato. The fragrance in the air from the knees-down consisted of the stench of old beer, urine, and an occasional whiff of vomit. I wandered around the Square and narrow streets for hours. It was clear that I was in the midst of a grand tourist destination. There was so much to take in.

I am not drawn to the normal tourist destinations. I love to get to know the locals and to step into the world outside of the tourist attractions. I like quaint. My favorite trips have involved things like borrowing some neighbor's, second-cousin's beater-car and heading out into the countryside. And hopping onto ferries and joining in sing-a-longs in tiny Irish Pubs. And staying in caravans where you have to drag the mattress outside to beat the dust out of it with a broom. I love all of that. I'm very grateful that Adara wants to go off the beaten path and explore.

The next morning we set out to find the Charles Bridge which crosses the Vitava River and takes us from Prague to "Lesser Town." Map in hand, Adara was on a mission to lead us to Prague Castle. Having experienced her as a "knowing" guide in Amsterdam, I was anticipating a very long walk. But I was definitely up for the experience. We quickly found out that we were only about a mile from the Charles Bridge. Walking across it was spectacular. The bridge was constructed in the fourteenth and fifteenth-centuries. It is about a quarter-mile long, and is lined with statues on either side that towered over us. The bridge surface itself is cobblestone and the bridge is constructed out of large old stone blocks. We maneuvered among the many artist booths and tables. As we strolled, I could imagine walking across the bridge on a snowy, winter night under the tall lantern lights. The thought gave me tingles up and down my spine.

We found our way to Lesser Town which was much quainter than the main Square. I wanted to enjoy the shops, sit at a patio, watch the people and get a sense of their culture, and take it all in, but Adara was still on a mission to get up to that damn castle. Needless to say, it was a very long day and the temperature was a balmy and humid ninety-four degrees. We walked and we walked and we walked. At the top of the hill I would have gone right to the castle but nope we went left. We never did make it to that castle but we slept really great that night. What was truly amazing though, was the view from the top of the hill and looking out over the greater area of Prague. It was enormous, shockingly enormous. There was nothing quaint about it!

I think it was day two or three when we learned of a defiant and political artist in Prague. His name is David Černý. Props to Adara, for doing all of the reading and research to lead the way to find as many of his well-known sculptures as we could. And finding them was not an easy task but made the adventure really fun. Now there was a free tour that would take us to all of the locations to see his work and could be completed in about an hour and a half. Nope, nope, nope, we did it Adara's way and with guide map in hand we set out each day to find the next Černý treasure. There were many times during our days together in Prague that I gently suggested another route to our destinations, but the cold stare I received reminded me of the wise words of my mentor, Wayne Dyer, who often said "You can be right or you can be happy." I chose happy! And I always love a great adventure.

The first sculpture we found was *Metalmorphosis*, which is a giant head of Franz Kafka staring into City Hall. The sculpture is positioned near where Kafka worked as an employee. Černý said that it is to remind us of Kafka when we are "Totally frustrated by the incompetence of state employees." It is a forty-five ton sculpture that is in constant motion, made up of spinning metal plates, and is mesmerizing to watch. The next of David Černý's sculptures that we found were *Peeing Guys* which were incredibly entertaining. We found these two naked guys right outside of the Franz Kafka Museum; two life-sized men holding their penises, with hips rotating, and peeing into a small pool the shape of the

Czech Republic. They were spelling out quotes from famous Prague residents. You could even send an SMS and they would personalize your message in urine. *Too much fun!*

Over the course of the next few days we walked, walked more, and eventually found more of Černý's art. We found *The Crawling Babies* at Kampa Park. Their faces are indented and down the front of their faces they have what appears to be a barcode. Nameless, faceless, babies. I never learned the significance for Černý of these giant, bronze babies but I suspect they capture the nameless, facelessness of our barcoded-society. We continued on and were under the impression that we had found *The Hanging Man* (Sigmund Freud) and checked that off of our list. But later upon closer examination of my photos, we did not see *The Hanging Man*. The photos I took clearly showed a business man with a briefcase hanging fifteen or twenty feet in the air from an umbrella on a steel line running between two buildings. I have no idea who the artist was, or the story, but I was fairly certain that I would not share my discovery with Adara. My favorite sculptures, which were the most difficult to find, were named *Brownnosing*. These two sculptures are now a permanent exhibit at the Futura Gallery, a small inconspicuous, very hard to find little gallery in Smichov. I fell in love with David Černý here. He is my kind of artist. These two sculptures must measure twenty feet tall to the top of their bums. They are standing bent over with their heads to the wall. They are each equipped with a ladder that you can climb up and stick your head in their bums. With your head inside each bum, you watch a video depicting two politicians, one feeding the other what looks like pablum that's running down the chin of the one being fed. The song *We Are the Champions* is playing on the video. It was outrageously funny! There were Černý masterpieces that we didn't see but we definitely enjoyed the ones we saw.

Within three blocks of our Airbnb there were three Jewish synagogues. Adara is Jewish and wanted to see each of them. I was delighted to go. I have not had much exposure to Jewish beliefs and traditions. The synagogues were fascinating, very small, and full of historical facts and photographs. The context however was a little unnerving. I had not realized the level of security that exists around the world at Jewish synagogues. Armed guards had a huge presence. It was sad to acknowledge the antisemitism that still exists in the world today. We then went outside to walk through the Jewish cemetery. I have been too hundreds of cemeteries but I had never seen a cemetery like this one. It was a small in-city cemetery, jam-packed full of headstones. There were headstones leaning over one another, headstones crammed in and resting on each other; broken, moss-covered headstones. Some of the headstones had little rocks on top of them symbolizing visits from loved ones. There was an area on one side of the cemetery with a sign that read "Fragments of Gothic Tombstones from mid-14th Cent." In that area there were little pieces of paper containing messages, folded up, and placed under little rocks. There were also thousands of little notes that were stuck right into crevices on the tombstones. I was very moved and emotional walking around and photographing there. For me there was a feeling of unrest. Even the cemetery was surrounded by a high chain-link fence, topped with barbed-wire, and armed guards were present.

There were a few occasions in Prague where I suddenly felt overwhelmed with strong emotions and like bursting into tears. One afternoon, while we were taking a breather inside our Airbnb, we heard crowds yelling, screaming, and chanting. I looked out the window and saw armed police on foot on both sides of the street and police vehicles going down the middle of the street to the Square. I looked at Adara and asked "Should we go see what's going on?" She replied with a resounding "Yes, let's go see." We walked down the street toward the Square and could see the crowd was moving quickly toward us. I thought it was some kind of political protest. I was videotaping with my phone and one of the protestors grabbed my phone, laughed, and then handed it back to me. We were amidst police, guns, dogs, and lots of yelling and chanting people. I felt overcome with emotion. We continued down the block to the Square and by the time we arrived all that remained were empty beer bottles and trash, and business appeared to be returning to normal. I wandered over to a restaurant and found someone who could speak enough English to tell me what had happened. I asked if it was a political protest and he said "No, no, no, there is futbol match tonight, Serbia and Czechia. Those were Serbian fans. It is normal fun." I must admit that I was relieved to hear that. That evening, Adara went to a symphony at one of the Jewish synagogues and I went to the Square, ate pizza, and watched the futbol game on a television that the restaurant owners had set up outside on the patio. Serbia won. I felt quite content to be watching the match on television instead of being present at the stadium.

There was another time that I was absolutely overcome with emotion in Prague. We had set out to find the John Lennon Wall which we had learned was somewhere over in Lesser Town. The good thing was we equally enjoyed walking because we sure did a lot of it. The John Lennon Wall was extremely difficult to find. This time though, I stopped and asked several people, one of whom directed us to its hidden location. When we arrived there were many people present, some with spray cans of paint adding their own artistic contributions. I am not sure what it was that filled me with such emotion, probably a combination of the writings on the wall and the presence of the wall itself. "Don't sell your dreams." "Save the Humans." "Life is short, war is long." "One time, one love, one life." "Hey Jude." "Love the skin you are in." "Do what you love, love what you do." I'm sure some of it was the words, but there was also a feeling of something made right in the world with the survival of the John Lennon Wall. Political authorities had ordered it to be white-washed again and again, but it survives. To top off the experience there was a young man, maybe early forties, playing his guitar and singing Beatles favorites. He had a sign in his open guitar case that read "Need money to repair my time machine to go back to the 60's." I tossed in my contribution.

My time with Adara was coming to an end. I had enjoyed the experience. It had been full, fun, and blessed with a few unanticipated opportunities to examine aspects of my story. I also found myself extremely excited to be able return to my solo journey. I had about five weeks left to continue to sort out who I am, why I am, what I want, how I may serve, and how my story has been shaping my life in ways that prevent those things I ache for from happening. I was deeply grateful for the remaining time and I looked very forward to returning to the more quiet *awarefulness* adventure that I had been on. Adara was scheduled to fly home the next morning. I would stay at a hotel near the airport and fly the following morning from Prague via Warsaw to Szczecin, followed by a ninety-kilometer train ride to Kolobrzeg, Poland where I had pre-booked a twenty-eight day stay. Adara and I shared an Uber to the airport. We dropped her off, she and I said our good-byes, see-ya-soons, and then the driver took me to my hotel. I checked-in and felt this tremendous relief of *Ahhhhhhhhhhhhhhhh!* And I felt immense gratitude that I would sleep in a bed that night.

Be the change you want to see in the world.

Mahatma Gandhi

Chapter Eleven

Reflections

My flight was scheduled to depart at 9:30 a.m. and I had been advised to be at the airport at least two hours early. I was there promptly at 7:00 a.m., only to read on the departures board that my flight to Warsaw had been cancelled. You know what? I didn't give two shits that it had been cancelled. My only concern was finding a customer service person who spoke enough English to help me find another flight. The FLY Polish Airlines counter was closed and the gentleman I spoke with at the Information Counter directed me to a little window on the far back wall with a sign above it that read FLY Polish Airlines. I wandered over to the far back wall and got in line behind two other people. There were two representatives behind two small windows in a tiny little office. Only one of them was helping those of us in line. I waited my turn. The two people in front of me seemed to be traveling together and it appeared that they were wrapping up and I was next. I had been in the short line for about forty-five minutes when a couple approached and got in line at the window where the representative was not helping anyone. He just kept his window closed and didn't make eye contact. From the sound of their accents, I think the couple that just arrived was speaking Russian. As soon as the people in front of me were finished, the Russian woman stepped in front of me and started speaking with the representative. I tapped her shoulder and said mostly in pantomime, "Excuse me, but it's my turn, I have been here a long time." She couldn't have cared less. Life appeared to be all about her. And you know what, I didn't care. I was happy to watch their exchange. It was moments like these that I was truly grateful to be traveling alone. I roll with these situations much easier than most. I had a little glint of what the scenario would be like if Adara was supposed to be on the same flight with me. I had a flash of a full-on brawl with Adara sitting on top of the Russian woman and squeezing her head in a vice grip. I actually laughed out loud.

It was finally my turn and I handed my flight itinerary to the woman behind the window, pointed to my flight numbers, and said "My flight was cancelled, can you help me?" She grabbed my paperwork and slammed the little window. She spent some time on her computer and then opened the window and said, "Only one flight is FLY Polish Airlines, only one I help with." I replied "No, both flights are FLY Polish Airlines and I pointed to each of the flight numbers." She slammed the window. I was aching inside from laughter. *Honestly.* About twenty minutes later she opened the window and handed me my new flight information. I would have a five-hour wait in Prague for my new forty-five minute flight to Warsaw, followed by another five-hour wait in Warsaw and a forty-five minute flight to Szczecin. I said "Thank you." She pointed in the direction of the FLY check-in counter and said "Go check bag now." There was actually a representative at the counter by then. I walked over and said "Hallo," handed the woman my new flight information, gestured toward the woman behind the window, and said "She told me to come check my bag now." Her reply "No! Too soon." I explained that my flight had been cancelled and she replied "So! Who tell you come here?" I again pointed to the woman behind the window. The check-in representative picked up the phone and called the woman behind the window and said a lot of things that I didn't understand, but I clearly saw that she was not happy. I am not sure what was said, but she checked my bag, and I proceeded through security and found a little cozy corner to upload more photos and enjoy the moments of solitude. As I settled in I wondered if my case would actually make it to my destination. There was something about the Czech people that I thoroughly enjoyed. My master's degree in Interpersonal Communication Education would be *entirely irrelevant* here. I kept chuckling.

My flight to Warsaw was a breeze. I mean we're talking forty-five minutes, not a lot to write home about. Except I did take a lot of aerial photos of Poland on that flight; very fascinating terrain, a unique combination of arid and forested. During my five-hour wait in the Warsaw airport, I found myself getting really excited about my stay in Poland. It was all prepaid and I was scheduled to stay from August 8 through September 5, leaving a few days to see other dear friends in London before my flight home on September 9.

Cozied up in another corner of a restaurant, I caught myself reflecting on a trip I took to Poland in 2004. I had been visiting my best friend in Wales and then traveled to meet a friend from Seattle who had just arrived in Warsaw. He had been a suitor for the previous few years, but my first impression of him had been that he was a very *moany, groany* person, and I had no interest in dating him. Just before I left for Wales, he had called and asked me to join him in Poland to explore a new area of Europe together. I was truly shocked when I said "Yes, okay." Mind you, in the months leading up to this offer, he had resurfaced and taken me to a few museums, luncheons, and had been shockingly enjoyable. In response to my "yes," he shuffled his travel dates and I cut my stay in Wales short and flew to Warsaw where we met at the airport and spent the day exploring before catching a train to Krakow. That was my first trip to Eastern Europe (or Central Europe depending on who you ask and the historical time-frame). I was about to fall in love with the Polish people and with Krakow.

That trip was the first experience I'd had being truly immersed in a non-English speaking culture. It was really different than any of my other experiences traveling in Western Europe, and very enjoyable indeed. I was initially happy to have a travel partner because we could put our heads together to decipher what the travel boards, signage, menus, and people were saying. However, and most unfortunately, he was that "Ugly American" traveler. His behavior blew me away. He had traveled all over the world and I assumed that he wouldn't be *that guy*. You know, the Ugly American who speaks loud, doesn't want to learn about the culture he's in, and just wants to tell his ever-important stories. He had a very obtrusive presence and unfortunately, standing at six-foot, four-inches, he also had a very loud physical presence. His drone of "I'm too tall, the seat is too small, my legs are cramped," lasted until he was certain that everybody had heard him. On our third day we took a train from Krakow to Zakopane, which I refer to as the Whistler of Poland. The train ride, *Oh my God.* Our reserved seats were in the same cabin as these two twenty-something year old Irish lads. They were funny and animated, very engaging, and started to share stories of where they were from and what life was like, when Kvetch (fitting name I've given him wouldn't you say?) interrupted and started to share his "hitchhiking" story from forty years ago. He completely silenced the young men and told his boring story for two hours of an almost three-hour train ride. I went to the dining car. The lads followed. I suspect that Kvetch kept telling his story in our absence. On our next travel day, and for the remainder of our time in Poland, I asked him to buy anything, anything whatsoever to read and advised him that I would be sitting in the seat furthest away from him.

I continued to love Poland and her people. We had arrived back in Krakow but had not yet found a place to stay. When commanded by Kvetch to "Let him handle it," I took a walk and found a pub in the Jewish Quarters and thoroughly enjoyed observing and listening to the locals. They have a history that would give them every reason to be angry or vengeful, but instead my experience was of happy people, lovely people, wonderful hosts, and awesome fresh fruits, vegetables, and meals in general. Well, except for the huge spoonful of lard that I put in my mouth at breakfast one morning. *True story.* We had stayed at a bed and breakfast in Zakopane, and in the morning we sat at a picnic-style table with five or six other people. They were all already eating when I joined them. I went through the buffet line and filled my plate with lovely fresh fruits, two slices of bacon, and what I thought was a large round ball of mashed potatoes. As we were all visiting I put a large spoon of the mashed potatoes in my mouth. It wasn't potatoes, it was lard; *a huge giant grease ball*! I felt that it would be terribly rude to spit it out so I sat there with it in my mouth while it slowly melted. I can only imagine the look on my face. I can tell you that I skipped the after-breakfast hike due to the fact that I was pretty committed to the toilet for the next several hours. I never did learn why they have huge balls of lard on the buffet table.

With only a few days left, I shared with Kvetch that it was very important to me to see Auschwitz-Birkenau. I wasn't sure why I felt so called to go there, but Kvetch agreed and the following day we took a taxi to Auschwitz-Birkenau. That experience rocked my world. I am also not sure that too many, or any, people on the planet would describe visiting Auschwitz-Birkenau as a spiritual experience, but for me it was deeply moving and very spiritual.

We had gone to the train station early in the morning to sign up for a tour of Auschwitz, and were in line to do so, when a man approached us and in very broken English said "I take you for less zloty." So we hopped in his taxi. It was about an hour's drive. After we had traveled about ninety kilometers, the driver pulled up alongside a ditch near the back corner of a huge field and he instructed us to get out of the car, go through the opening in the fence, and asked "What time we meet at front gate?" Kvetch and I were confused, shrugged our shoulders, and said with a huge question mark on our faces, "An hour?" Agreed. We hadn't yet realized that we had just been dropped off at the far back corner of Birkenau, which consisted of four hundred and twenty-five acres of barbed-wire fences, towers, barracks, and an unforgettable smell of death. It didn't take us more than a few minutes to realize where we were. We wandered by the remnants of the four original large crematoria which had been destroyed by the SS at the end of World

War II. It still smelled of ashes, the ashes of mass murder. I wept as we walked along the cobblestone area which had been created as an international memorial to the persons who were murdered in the "death factory" at Auschwitz-Birkenau. I love photography and I walked around and shot several rolls of color film and then walked back around and shot several rolls of black and white film. I wish we would have said that we'd meet the driver in three hours. I don't have words to describe what it was like to be there and to feel the horror that took place on those four hundred and twenty-five acres. I guess the words disbelief, gut wrenching, excruciating sadness, and somber, kind of capture the feeling.

We headed toward the main gate. We weren't talking much. It was such an overwhelming experience to take in and to digest. We actually never saw another soul until we got close to the gate where we spotted a woman leading a small tour group. Our driver was there waiting for us and we got into the taxi and he said "Now we go Auschwitz." Birkenau is about three kilometers from Auschwitz. I was moved to my core at Birkenau and was totally unprepared for what was next. Again, our driver picked a time for us to meet him. This time we asked for three hours. Agreed. The main entrance to Auschwitz is a large, wrought-iron gate and across the top it reads "Arbeit Macht Frei," which means "work brings freedom." A perfect example of the lies that were told to the people who boarded the trains bound for Auschwitz.

After entering we were free to tour the various blocks. The block hallways were personalized with photographs of the men, women, and children who were taken prisoner. I was speechless. I walked through all of the blocks and took in the unimaginable. I saw the cellars where sterilization experiments on small children took place, and the death block with the killing wall, and the starvation cells. Block 5 contained all of the prisoners' personal belongings. Behind the first large glass encasement there were tens of thousands of pairs of eyeglasses, and behind another encasement there were thousands of crutches and artificial limbs. And another encasement contained suitcases with the prisoners' names, and sometimes dates and addresses. The last encasement contained tens of thousands of pairs of shoes. We learned that there used to be thirty warehouses of personal belongings that were destroyed by the SS. I was without words and didn't even attempt to try to stop the tears that were streaming down my cheeks. *What horror.* I actually thought that if everyone could visit Auschwitz-Birkenau, then maybe one day the citizens of the world would have a chance at world peace.

At the time we were scheduled to depart, I did not want to get into the taxi and leave. You might think this is the craziest thing you've ever heard, but I wanted to stay at Auschwitz for a day or two. I wanted to hide away until the tourists left. And I wanted to just be there in the quiet, unsettledness of it all. I felt a restless spiritual presence that felt like voices that wanted to be heard. I wanted to hear them. I wanted to give witness to their words. I wanted to help them. I feel the same overwhelming emotion even as I write these words. I wondered, "Was I a prisoner here?" "Was my family here?" My thoughts turned to my maternal roots; my grandparents' surname is Zachrich and my great grandparents' surname is Schmecel. My questions deepened, "Was I a guard?" "Did I do the killing?" What was unquestionable though was that I could feel the suffering. I felt enveloped in the memories of terror, anguish, and suffering. I could feel it at the core of my Being. I did not want to leave, but I will also never know what it would have been like to spend the night alone in one of the Blocks. I shared with Kvetch what I was feeling and he rolled his eyes at me. I had a fleeting thought of escorting him back to Block 11, the Death Block with the Killing Wall.

I have had other experiences in my life where I've found myself overwhelmed with emotion and memories not of this lifetime. For example, my first trip to Europe was in 1976 right after I graduated from high school. I went on a six-week trip with the Foreign Study League and our last stop was London. We were on a bus heading who knows where, and I was looking out the window at the neighborhood and the sidewalks and I was all of the sudden overwhelmed with emotion. Tears streamed down my cheeks. I absolutely recognized this place, and before we got to the corner I knew what we were going to see. I could have drawn a picture of the street before the bus turned the corner. I knew this place. I don't know what each of your belief systems are about life, death, past lives, or reincarnation. I stay curiously open. My belief testing system is very simple. Does what I am hearing, reading, or experiencing in any way resonate with my Being? Does it have a truth frequency for me? I personally think that my experience in London in 1976, and my experience in Auschwitz in 2004, are examples of past life merit. I understand that to mean that we successfully metabolized a level of consciousness, with memories intact, and we brought it forward into a next incarnation. Like déjà vu. My life is blessed with many.

> Your purpose boils down to what it is that you
> have to give back to the world and for that you
> need to know who you really are.

Deepak Chopra

Chapter Twelve

A Delightful Surprise

I looked up at the clock and it was almost time to head to my gate for my flight from Warsaw to Szczecin. Due to my anticipated very late arrival, earlier in the day I had emailed my booking representative and requested that she contact the hotel to make arrangements for a driver to pick me up and drive me the ninety kilometers to Kolobrzeg. I would arrive too late to catch the last train which I had planned to take.

As I gathered up my belongings it struck me what a coincidence it was that I had spent the last four hours in Warsaw reflecting on Auschwitz and the death camps, and how such an enormous part of this sojourn for me is to remember *Who I Really Am*, why I am, what I want, and how I may serve. My deepest driving desire for the past two decades has been to help people talk openly and easily about death and dying. This is a huge piece of what I hoped that my ninety-two days of self-reflection and introspection would shed some light on. My interest in death and dying is a profound part of my story, the story that I have been living, and my dharma as a teacher. And *be damned* if I have been able to figure out how to serve in this realm. I have gifts to share. Curiously open conversations about death and dying can bring tremendous healing to all of us and elevate our understanding of *Who We Really Are.*

I boarded my second forty-five minute flight of the day, another quick and easy, uneventful flight. I found my way to baggage claim, gathered my case, and spotted a man holding a sign with my hotel name written on it. I was quite delighted to see him. It was now 23:00 hours and I was ready to get to my destination. I figured that the drive would take about an hour and a half. My driver did not speak English but he would point out road signs to give me a gauge on our arrival time at the hotel. It was almost midnight and a full moon lit the fields and the hillsides as we passed by. It was an incredibly beautiful night. After about an hour into the drive, we turned off the main road and onto a dirt road that led into the woods. I must admit that I got a little unnerved. It flashed through my mind that I was not on the flights that were indicated on the itineraries that I left for my family, I was not on the train I should have been on, and now I was on a dirt road in the woods at midnight with a stranger and I had no idea where I was. I must have gasped in a deep breath that alerted the driver to turn to me and say "Road good, safe, soon hotel." I really appreciated his words and smiled. Within fifteen minutes we arrived and I went to the check-in desk, where I was greeted by a sweet woman who handed me a note that said, "Welcome Hawks come desk morning 7:00 for lady speak English." I smiled, nodded, and took the note and the key to my room. The driver was kind enough to carry my case up two flights of stairs and into my room. Why we didn't take the elevator I'm not sure. Maybe it was for the big tip.

It was a perfect little room with private bath and a balcony that looked out to the woods. I unpacked just enough to brush my teeth and to put on my pajamas. It was now 1:00 a.m. and I needed to be at the front desk at 7:00 a.m. I carefully chose this destination for the third part of my three-part journey. Part one, deep rest, detox, and nourishment. Check! Part two, waking-up and finding some energy again. Check! Part three, getting mentally, emotionally, and physically strong. When I was conducting my research and planning this adventure, I discovered that this area of Poland on the Baltic Sea was an extremely popular destination for healing and spa-treatment vacations. It totally fit the bill for me given the budget I was on and the length of time I would be staying. I prepaid for a twenty-eight day, all-inclusive, full-board package which included all meals and "twenty medically prescribed treatments per week Monday through Friday." Treatments "such as brine, peat and carbon dioxide bath, hydromassage, partial massage, mud and mud pack, laser, cryo-, electro-magnetic and galvanotherapy, ultrasound, iontophoresis, Solux lamp, inhalation, individual and group gymnastics, water gymnastics, ergometer, sling table." The total cost was $1,780 USD. Perfect. I had no idea what some of the treatments were but I was up for the taste test. I chose it for both the price and because I had fallen in love with the people of Poland in 2004. Twenty-eight days, I whispered to myself with a smile on my face as I fell into a deep sleep. But not before praying to God, Brahman, Allah, Buddha, Krishna, Mother Teresa, et al., the familiar crowd. I apologized for being a bit remiss with my prayers over the past twelve days while I was playing tourist. But I was back now to ask for guidance and to continue to examine my story and the thoughts that influenced my story.

My alarm went off at 6:00 a.m. It was Wednesday, August 9. I took a quick shower, got dressed, and went down to the front desk to talk with the lady who speaks English. When I was booking this part of my trip I had seen a disclaimer that read, "You must be able to speak Polish or German for the initial medical consultation." I clarified three times with the booking representative that I do not speak Polish or German and asked if that was going to be a problem. She checked with the hotel and confirmed that it would definitely not be a problem. She said that there were a couple of people to assist with translation and I could always use a translator program on my laptop. I met a delightful woman at the front desk. She spoke very broken English, and all I knew how to say in Polish was hello and thank you. I think I was instructed to go eat for five minutes and then go downstairs to meet with the doctor for my medical consultation. I did both.

The food was served buffet-style like it was in Marienbad but on a much, much smaller scale. I am not a picky eater, but the food was just okay. There were a couple selections of meats and cheeses, watermelon plates, hard boiled eggs, and a table with some box cereals and yogurt. I forgot to mention earlier that also included in my full-board package was free wine and beer at lunch and dinner. I didn't plan on enjoying much, if any, beer or wine at this point on my journey. It was my desire to continue to get healthy. After I finished breakfast I went downstairs, entered a short hallway, and sat in one of the seven old-school style chairs. They had tall, white metal backs with white legs and light-teal colored seats. There were five on one side of the hallway and two on the other side. I chose to sit in one of the two. I was only there about ten minutes when a woman approached me and said "Hallo," and spoke several quick sentences in Polish (*I think*) and walked into a nearby office. I followed, hoping that I was supposed to follow. I introduced myself and said that I speak English and do not speak Polish or German. She had paperwork in front of her and her goal was to conduct my medical consultation and design my treatment program for the duration of my stay. We were not making much progress with our combination of charades and pantomime. After several awkward moments she stood up and said "Colleague English," and she walked out of the small office into the hallway. I waited. *I think I was supposed to wait.*

Within five minutes the doctor/consultant was back with a male colleague. He sat on a chair to the left of me and said "Hallo, I speak English. I help with you understand." I chuckled to myself and wondered how good his English really was. The moment felt like I was in store for another wonderful adventure. I had previously made some notes and shared them with "the colleague." I emphasized that I wanted to take aquafit classes every day, exercise every day, and have massages, mud packs, and whatever additional treatments they recommended of the buffet of treatments offered at the hotel.

I shared that I had had lower back surgery twenty-two years ago and five years ago, and that yoga, walking, and meditation keep me healthy and pain free. After every few sentences that I spoke, the colleague who I had not been formally introduced to, would translate for the doctor. She scribbled lots of notes, then looked at her colleague and said, "Okay, you go." The colleague turned to me and said "I teach aquafit and do massages." I asked him if I could go to aquafit class that morning. He replied "Yes, I teach three classes at 8:00, 8:30, and 9:00." It was now 8:35 and I asked if I could go get my swimsuit and come to class now. He said "yes." I ran up to my room, put my swimsuit on, realized that there were no robes and only a hand towel, so I grabbed the hand towel and ran back down the stairs to the lower level to the pool.

I popped in and out of the pre-pool shower and went out to the pool. There were only three or four people in the class, a mix of men and women, again about the age of my parents. The pool at the deep end was about three feet deep, a bit of a disappointment. Since the colleague had told me that he taught three classes at 8:00, 8:30, and 9:00, I assumed they were pretty short classes. I had been prepped for that in Marienbad. So far on this grand adventure I have had yoga, aquafit, and Nordic walking classes taught in German, Czech, Russian, and now in Polish; except this instructor did not say anything. He was my first mime instructor! Like all of the aquafit instructors that I've had on this sojourn, he stayed outside of the pool to lead the class. I could feel the laughter brewing inside of me. Since arriving late to the 8:30 class I decided to stay for the 9:00 class. I was fairly certain that I wasn't going to over exert myself. In between the classes, when I was the only one in the pool, the "colleague" came over to the side of the pool and motioned for me to come. I walked over and he held out his hand and said "My name is Żądza." I shook his hand and said "Nice to meet you Żądza, my name is Cait. Thank you for helping with the consultation." He smiled. I wasn't certain that he understood a word I said.

Like the 8:30 class, the 9:00 class was also taught in mime. Żądza was standing at the end of the pool and to the left, and I caught myself looking up at him and thinking, "Hmmm, this guy is pretty hot. I wonder how old he is, quite tasty indeed." There were three of us in this class and one of the women was young with young children who were playing in the even more, shallow end of the pool. I was delighted to see that there was an age range here. At the end of the 9:00 class I stayed in the pool and was going to do my own workout. Żądza, again motioned for me to come to the side of the pool. I thought he was going to make me leave the pool because he was finished teaching the day's classes and there was no lifeguard. Instead, he was advising me of my treatment schedule. He said "Tomorrow at 17:00 you have massage with hot rocks." I was delighted. I asked where I could pick up my daily schedule and he instructed me to go to the front desk later that day. "Perfect. Can I stay in the pool right now?" He nodded yes and left.

After another thirty minutes of alone time in the pool, I went up to my room and changed. I stopped at the front desk to ask for directions to the ocean which I could not see because the hotel was surrounded by forest. After pantomiming ocean waves, surfing, and swimming, the lovely lady at the front desk pointed in the direction I should head. This was my first time actually seeing where I was in daylight. I loved the remote location. It was just as charming as the online photos I had seen when I chose this particular hotel. As I walked around the corner of the property I saw a row of bikes and spent about ten minutes trying to figure out what the heck the directions said to be able to unlock and use a bike. I gave up and went on my walk. I figured that I could ask Żądza for his help later.

As I set out on the path toward the ocean I was absolutely amazed at the size and sophistication of the paths, and by all of the activity on them. There were young and old people, babies in strollers, bikers, walkers, skate boarders, and others riding scooters. I was truly stunned. There were portable outhouses called Toi Toi's and path signs as sophisticated as highway signage; signs pointing to Ustronie Morskie, to Kolobrzeg, and to Podczele. I had heard that I was about eight kilometers from Kolobrzeg and I wanted to spend some time there. I walked the path to the ocean and was surprised that there were very few people on the beach at that time in the morning. The beach stretched in each direction to the horizon. I walked and took pictures for an hour or so. On my way back to the trailhead that spit me out onto the beach, I saw young families arriving in droves. Many were opening up what looked like large wicker chests, which when opened, folded out to these sweet covered chairs with footstools. I had never seen anything like them. There were also portable panels made out of nylon and wood sticks that you could use to mark off your territory or make your own private enclosure. I had one of those in my hotel room but could not for the life of me figure out what it was. *Now I know*!

I wandered back down the paved path to my hotel. It was just about lunchtime. I turned and walked across the lawn to the back of the hotel which I had not seen yet. It was outstanding. The back of the property was comprised of a large meadow full of wild heather and surrounded by ancient pine trees, and there were old-school, wood and iron tables and chairs sitting in the grass. Nearer to the hotel was a big patio with white tables, umbrellas, and chairs. *Simple awesomeness*. I was really happy to be here.

I sat in the grassy area on a wooden chair and soaked in the sun for about twenty minutes. I reflected on my thoughts that shape my story and how I've saved examining the most important aspects of my story for this third portion of my *awarefulness* journey; to explore my dharma and to deepen my awareness of *Who Am I? Why Am I?* What do I want? How may I serve? What is the conversation that I most want to participate in and who can most benefit? I'm not sure how or when I became most fascinated with endings and with death, but I have been consciously aware of this calling for twenty-five years.

Twenty-five years I have been knocking on doors trying to find the like-minded people who know the healing value of talking about death and dying. Twenty-five years of trying to find my venue, my tribe, and to discover how to make my contribution to the collective consciousness. At the time I departed on this sojourn I had grown very weary and could not figure out how, with whom, and for whom to offer my gifts. I have knocked on doors, I have meditated on it, I have prayed, and I have tried on hats and played a variety of professional roles. Still, I hadn't found my venue.

When I have ignored this calling it swells up inside of me and chokes me. My greatest fear for the past few decades has been the fear of dying with my music still inside of me. As soon as I mention my interest in teaching others to talk with ease about death and dying, the vast majority of people direct me to hospice and to palliative care. I used to be a little taken aback by that but I understand it now. These contexts are the ones that we have determined to be appropriate to have conversations on death and dying. We have assigned the conversations to medical professionals, who often have little or no training in interpersonal conversations about death and dying. My interest is in exploring these conversations at early ages. I think that courses in discussions of death and dying should exist as a pre-requisite for all bachelor degree programs. I think there should be a series of required courses in all medical schools. The taboo and the darkness that surround these conversations still permeate the larger societal consciousness. *But we are all going to die!* I think it is worth our while to explore what that means. What is death? What dies?

I don't know how we can achieve our own conscious evolution without exploring our concepts of death and dying and without exploring why we belief what we believe. And I continue to pray to God et al. for guidance. How can I accomplish my goals? There have been some shifts in consciousness over the past decade surrounding conversations on death and dying. I have knocked on doors of some of the most advanced thinkers in the field of palliative care. I have heard "We just don't have a need for your services at this time." *How can that be?* I suspect that I butt up against their fears and as such feel silenced by those fears.

Off to lunch. The room was alive with accents, mostly Polish I believe. The lunchroom was brimming with young families. It was quite delightful. I filled my plate with a few slices of oranges, watermelon, rice, and something? The meal was just mediocre. The watermelon tasted a bit like vinegar. It wasn't great food. Of course there was free beer and wine. I had a sip of wine, it was not great wine. I finished eating and wandered into the front lobby area. I stopped at the front desk and asked if my schedule was ready to pick up. They had no idea what I was saying so I thought it best to just check back later. I went into the lounge area, took photos, and then sat in one of the old, overstuffed chairs and just people watched. Then Żądza walked in and said "I look for you." I responded "Well here I am." I asked him if he could show me how to rent the bikes. He said yes. I asked him if he could show me the best way to get to Kolobrzeg. He said yes. He went on to say that my massage "Maybe today, maybe tomorrow." I replied that either day was just fine. Then, as he turned to leave, Żądza said "I come with car today at 4:00 for you." "Okay, but I'm not sure I understand why." He said "We go to Kolobrzeg, I take you." *Awesome!*

I went on another walk. This time I walked along the path in the opposite direction from my earlier walk to see what the neighborhood was like. It was 2:00 p.m. which gave me two hours before Żądza would be coming to pick me up. It was an old-world neighborhood consisting of apartment homes, some single family residences, little hot dog and ice cream stands, and a small general store. I adore small general stores. I grew up with those in Calgary. I went inside and lingered for close to an hour trying to figure out what everything was. Fruits, vegetables, meats, and cheeses are obvious, but most everything canned or wrapped is just fun. I bought some cough drops and two protein bars, *I think?* I walked back to the hotel and still had about half an hour. I went to the lounge and ordered a glass of wine. It was no better than the sip I had at lunch. I think it was just a sign that I can cleanse my life of drinking. As I sat waiting for 4:00 p.m. to approach, I had the thought that maybe I should run up to my room and get my driver's license and put it in a pocket, or a sock, or my underwear just in case this hot, seemingly-nice man is a crazed murderer. If he were, who would ever have a chance of finding me? I checked in with my gut feeling and I wasn't getting any be scared for your life signals. Plus, I wasn't even sure if I really understood him correctly or whether he would be coming to pick me up at all. At 4:00 p.m. I went out to the front steps of the hotel and Żądza was just pulling up in his car. I hopped in and off we went.

I asked where we were going and he replied "To Kolobrzeg, I will show you bikes and massage with hot rocks." We visited while he drove and exchanged information about ourselves. He asked me where I was from and I simply replied "Canada." I thought saying Calgary, Alberta, Canada would be too confusing. He was delighted that I was from Canada. I was his "First Canadian to meet." Then I asked him where he was from and he said "1970." I choked down my laughter, then did a quick calculation in my head, and thought to myself "Thank God he's older than my daughter." He was nine years older than my daughter and twelve years younger than me.

Żądza was light natured and we laughed easily. We arrived in Kolobrzeg and he pointed out a few places that are "Good to come back and visit." Then we drove into a gated complex and he parked and said "Follow me, my place." I was a little surprised but still had no bad gut feeling and happily followed. We went up a couple flights of stairs to his little flat. There in the middle of the room was a massage table, and on the floor, a crockpot filled with medium-sized, flat, black rocks. He looked at me with a beaming smile and said "See like I say massage with hot rocks." I was totally taken aback and replied "*Ohhhhhhhhh*, you take me to Kolobrzeg and I have a massage with hot rocks *here!*" All the pieces of what he had been trying to share with me came together in that moment. He nodded and said "*Yes!*" I asked "Right now?" "Yes."

I looked around the small flat and didn't see a changing area so I just bucked up and took off my clothes, dropped them on the kitchen floor, and crawled up onto the table. And I thought "Good thing I didn't hide my driver's license in my panties." Now I have never done anything like this before in my entire life. Well, not in Poland. Truthfully, I have been one of the shyest people on the planet when it comes to getting naked in front of anyone ever! I used to get detention in high school gym class because I would not get naked and shower after class. I am still the girl in the shower room before aquafit classes that gets changed in the toilet stall instead of out in the open with everyone else. I have just always been insanely shy naked or in a bathing suit. I guess I've healed that problem. I am fifty-nine years old and dropped my clothes off right in that little kitchen and thought "OK so this is what's going on."

Żądza had rubbed heated oil on his hands and was massaging my back. It felt amazing after my long travel-day the day before. *Holy shit*, it occurred to me that I had just arrived late last night and here I was having this experience. And I thought I was in trouble last night when the driver went off the main road onto the dirt road into the woods at midnight. Now I was naked in a stranger's flat having a massage. *Cait has been unleashed!* I didn't have a *flippin* care in the world. I felt awake and alive and utterly irresponsible. It was a very delicious feeling indeed. I had married at nineteen years old and had given birth to my daughter just five days before my first anniversary. All I have ever known is how to be utterly responsible. I guess I have healed that gene.

I had been enjoying the full-body massage for about twenty minutes when I thought I felt a kiss on my lower back, then another on my right shoulder, and another on my left shoulder. I was completely surprised and started to tense up. Then I said to myself "Oh just relax girl and go with it, you're in Poland with Mr. Hot man." I sank into the experience which was so seductive and fabulous. Then a kiss on the top of my right buttocks and then on my left, and Żądza said "You have a supaw bottom." I did not utter a word. He continued with my deliriously, excellent massage; then I felt the wisp of his fingertips up close and personal between my inner thighs. He asked me to turn over and looked to me for permission to continue. He had my permission. He had me at "supaw." My only thought was "He's so handsome and I'm really enjoying this sweet surprise." He climbed onto the table . . . . It was such a sturdy little table.

Fifteen minutes later, I was again lying on my stomach while he placed these fabulous hot rocks up and down each side of my spine. I lay there wearing a Mona Lisa smile with visions of Żądza running through my mind. I don't know what "hot" means to you when it comes to male attractiveness, but here's what "hot" looks like on this man. He's six-foot, three-inches tall, very lean and athletic, dark brown smiling eyes, dark hair with graying sideburns, almost a baby face, but with a bit of ruggedness and a dimpled-chin. His ease and laughter added to his physical attractiveness. *Yum, yum.* I have chosen the name Żądza for him because that is the Polish word for lust. *Uh huh.*

We sat on his little balcony and drank tea. He said he would take me back soon, which he did. I laid in bed that night reflecting on the whole experience and thanked Mother Teresa for that delightful event. I am sure it was a gift from her. What woman doesn't ache at times to feel desirable, beautiful, and sexy? *Done.* I must have worn that well-laid look on my face for several days.

I went down to the front desk first thing in the morning in hopes that my daily treatment schedule would be available. *Walah*, it was there. I could go to aquafit classes and then my first treatment was at 10:00 a.m. I had a quick bite to eat. The food had not improved. I had planned to go to the aquafit classes but decided at the last minute not to. I wasn't sure what it would be like to see Żądza, and quite frankly, I just wanted to cherish the exquisite memory. The man is an extremely talented masseuse, the kind that fantasies are made up of, and in this case came true. I did go downstairs for my first treatment though. I sat in one of those old-school, hallway chairs where several other people were also sitting. They each had a thin blue large piece of fabric folded in their laps. I touched the folded fabric in the lap of the person sitting next to me and asked "Where did you get?" She turned her head away. Then a tall young man with a clipboard in hand called my name. I think it was my name. It is pretty hard to screw up Cait. I stood up and followed him into a little room.

I was feeling both excited and ambivalent about the treatments and the facilities. My focus for these twenty-eight days was to get physically strong. So far the pool depth was a disappointment, as was the very strong smell of chlorine. There was no exercise room at all and no exercise classes on the schedule. I was hoping that the twenty treatments per week were the hotel program's strong point. Of course there were always the bikes and miles and miles of walking trails. The small treatment room contained four hospital-type dividers on wheels which served to separate the four little treatment areas. I could see that there were people lying face up behind each of the four partitions. The partitions looked like something out of a MASH unit. The young man pointed to a little narrow bed up against one of the walls and gestured for me to get on it. I asked "Massage?" He nodded yes. I asked "Take clothes off?" He nodded yes. I was fairly certain that he did not understand a single word that I said. I studied the table for a second and it seemed unusually low for a massage table, so I decided to just take off my shoes and lay down on the little bed. He nodded. Thank God I opted to keep my clothes on. I wouldn't want to give a wrong impression like I'm easy or something ridiculous like that.

After I lay down, he slid this round, donut-shaped apparatus up my legs and aligned it over my waste, hit a button, and left the room. The apparatus made x-ray type sounds. I have no idea what it was. After about ten minutes the young man came back, turned off the machine, and took me to the neighboring small room with similar MASH unit partitions. This time I could see that the other people behind the partitions all had their shirts off. He motioned for me to take my shirt off and lay down on my stomach, and I obliged. Then he put these two flat, round, conductor-type things on my back and turned on a little machine. He asked if it was good. I couldn't feel a thing but suspected that I should at least feel a tiny current. I stayed there for ten minutes. He returned, turned off the machine, and I put my shirt back on. He pointed to "lunch" on the schedule and then to "massage" after lunch. I nodded. He pointed to himself and then again to "massage" on the schedule and said "with me." I suspected that it wouldn't even remotely compare to the massage I had the day before.

I went upstairs to the lunchroom where I really hoped to find more nourishing food than the previous meals. I served myself a bowl of soup (*I think*), a salad, and watermelon. I had just sat down to eat when Żądza walked up to my table with his lunch tray in hand. I sheepishly greeted him. He said "You miss my class, why?" I told him that I had slept in. He asked me if I would like another hot rock massage. I replied "Oh no thank you. It was very good but no thank you." His mouth fell open in shock! Don't misunderstand, the man is excellent at his "special" massages, but my feeling was how do you top the last one and how do you top the element of surprise. It had been over-the-moon outstanding. I simply wanted to cherish the memory and the shit-eating grin that I was still wearing on my face. We sat, ate lunch, and visited. Mine was no better tasting than the other meals. Before Żądza left he took out his phone and said "We trade phone numbers." As we were entering each other's numbers, he asked "What is your name?" We looked each other in the eyes and broke into outrageous laughter. I thought about saying "Supaw, last name Bottom." We said goodbye and I told him I would see him in aquafit class the next morning. As he was leaving Żądza shared that he had friends coming into town in two days that would be staying at his small flat and that he would "Come and sleep with me for five days." I am certain that he meant stay with me but I chuckled out loud. I nodded affirmatively but wondered if I wanted to share my room for five days.

I went for a long walk before my scheduled massage with the man who had rendered my morning treatments. As I walked I was tapping into this strong feeling that this program may not fit the bill for the third portion of my sojourn. After my walk I decided to send an email to my booking representative to express my disappointment in the facilities, the lack of fitness programs, the treatments which were not even remotely on a scale of what I had hoped for, and the food pretty basically sucked. I thought about sharing that they do have a person on staff that gives spectacular special massages, but I elected not to. I did share with her that I would like to book another place and do it quickly if my prepayment could be applied elsewhere. She confirmed that the sooner I made that decision, the better. I authorized her to speak with the hotel manager and began my search for another program. When I was in Schwabisch Hall researching next destinations, I had almost booked another place in Germany instead of going to Marienbad and I immediately researched it again. I decided that I wanted to leave and gave my booking representative my blessing to book Hotel Tannenbaum in Bad Wörishofen on my behalf. It was Friday and she asked if I could be ready to leave as early as Monday. I told her I could be ready as early as the next morning but it was the weekend and I would have to wait until Monday. It was the end of her workday when we spoke and she said that she would call Hotel Tannenbaum first thing Monday morning.

I went downstairs for my massage appointment. Much to my surprise Żądza was sitting in one of the hallway chairs, and as I approached and said "Hallo," he stood up and motioned for me to come into a small room with a massage table. I asked "You are giving me a massage?" He smiled and said "Yes, I got it changed to me, for you." I shook my head, smiled, entered the room, and took off my clothes. I was wondering how this was going to go. I assumed it would be very professional because he was at work, and it was, for the most part. Except for a few sweet kisses and a couple of whoopsie daisy slights of fingertips, it was a very short, tiny bit seductive, intimate, and teasing fifteen minute massage. Żądza stayed in the room while I got dressed and asked "Now you come for second hot rock massage?" I shook my head, flashed him a smile, and said "Yes please." He picked me up at 5:00 p.m. We went to his flat. *That is just the most amazing sturdy little massage table ever made.* And that Mona Lisa smile was back. On our return to the hotel I told Żądza that I was not going to continue my stay at the hotel and that I was checking out other programs. He seemed a bit upset and sad, and said "No you say you stay for twenty-eight days." Without wanting to disrespect where he worked, I simply said that I needed a program where I could get really strong and healthy. He told me that there were many hotels in Kolobrzeg that have good programs and I definitely agreed to check them out.

The next morning I looked at my treatment schedule and it was the same as the previous day. I opted out. Instead I walked to the beach and then walked eight kilometers down the beach to Kolobrzeg. The closer I got to town the more crowded the beach was. It was really quite extraordinary. This area is a vacation haven for Polish families. When I arrived at the edge of the town I walked up from the beach to the paved paths. Again, I was impressed with the very sophisticated trail system. I saw a man darting off quickly on a side trail into the woods. I decided to follow and see where it led. I shouldn't have. It led to him dropping his trousers and making a deposit in the woods. Right back to the main trail I went chuckling the whole way. I walked a little further and a woman and child went off the beaten path and I followed them. Again, I shouldn't have. She pulled off her little girl's pants and held her waist high with little legs spread and a stream of urine shooting my direction. Back to the main path I went. I was laughing out loud this time. I was also starting to suspect that the Toi Tois were for out-of-country travelers who were not as accustomed to darting off the main path to keep the forest lands fertilized.

I went into one of the hotels that was part of the same group of hotels as the one I was currently staying at, and which offered health and wellness programs. It was much nicer. There was a great fitness room. The pool was twice the size with classes every day. The treatment schedule looked great. I toured the whole facility and was giving serious thought to staying put in Poland. It would be so much easier to move eight kilometers from my current hotel versus rebooking flights and traveling to Hotel Tannenbaum. I wandered back outside to meet Żądza. He had said he would meet me there after he finished work. We went upstairs to an outside café and drank lemonade and talked. He offered to drive me to

Gdansk or Krakow to check out other places. I told him that I thought I found the one that will be best for me and that it was in Bavaria about eighty kilometers west of Munich. I was very surprised how affected he seemed. He called a taxi to take me back to my hotel. He rode his bike to his flat.

I attended all three aquafit classes the next morning. They were marvelous. Mr. Mime was in true form, adding pool ballroom dancing to his repertoire of aquafit instruction. *Fun stuff.* I elected not to continue with any of the other treatments. Instead I sat in the backyard meadow on one of the wooden chairs reflecting on my past few days in Poland. I caught myself laughing out loud as I looked at the treatment descriptions on my "all-inclusive" stay paperwork. I wondered what the donut-shaped apparatus was. Maybe that was the "electro-magnetic" therapy? Maybe I was radiated? I think that the little round metal things placed on my back were likely a form of ultrasound. I had seen something similar in a Chiropractor's office decades ago. I broke into an out-loud belly laugh when I thought about the hot rock massages. Maybe they were "partial massage" combined with "group gymnastics," on a "sling table." Well, one thing for certain was that my experience with Żądza was not his first rodeo. There was a serious level of skilled excellence there and I'm sure it took a lot of practice. Just his ability to mount the table was impressive as hell. My cheeks were again aching from laughter.

The next day, Żądza and his little dog Yeti, picked me up and we drove to another beach. We parked and walked a few blocks past food vendors, face painters, Shetland pony rides, and all kinds of carnival fun. It was Sunday and I would be leaving the next day, flying from Szczecin via Warsaw to Munich. Żądza had offered to drive me the ninety kilometers from Kolobrzeg to Szczecin. I accepted. He said he still didn't understand my decision to leave and he offered to help me get strong. It was a very tempting offer. But I thought to myself how I really needed to get a lot more than just my inner-thigh and glute muscles strong. I didn't have the heart to tell him that meeting a guy for crazy, hot sex was just delicious, but that I had a lot more self-reflecting to do on this sojourn. He and Yeti spent the night.

Żądza went to teach his morning classes and then at 11:30 a.m. we loaded my cases in his car and off we went. I was learning that his command of the English language was not even remotely as good as he thought it was. The things that we could easily understand, outside of hot rock massages, were movie titles and movie stars' names. We had quickly discovered that we shared a mutual love for great movies. The drive was easy with lots of hysterical laughter. On the way to Szczecin he pulled off into the woods and ran down a path. I suspected I knew why. I did not follow. We arrived at the airport, Żądza took my cases out of the trunk, gave me a big hug, and said "I will come to North America and visit you for two weeks or one year." Then he hopped back in his car, waved, and drove away. It was a very quick goodbye.

Travel brings power and love back into your life.

Rumi

Chapter Thirteen

The Road to Getting Strong

From Szczecin I would have a flight change in Warsaw, and would be arriving in Munich late. I had no idea how I was getting from Munich to Hotel Tannenbaum in Bad Wörishofen. It would involve a couple of train changes. I booked a hotel for the night near the airport in Munich. When I arrived at my hotel, a lovely front-desk person drew out explicit directions for me for travel to Bad Wörishofen the next morning. Three trains and I would be there. It was an uneventful night in comparison to the previous night with Żądza. I slept wonderfully, and the next morning I decided that I did not have the desire for a day of train travel and I arranged an Uber. That was one of the most ridiculously expensive costs that I incurred during my entire ninety-two-day journey. And I didn't have a single moments regret. It was an outstanding way to travel. Hotel Tannenbaum did not have a room available for two days, so I stayed at another hotel for the first few nights. I arrived in Bad Wörishofen on August 15, and would stay until September 5. I felt really great about my decision to change my plans. Hotel Tannenbaum was $800 USD more expensive than the hotel and program in Poland. And I was hoping it was worth the change. This third getting strong portion of my journey was extremely important to me.

I explored the hotel where I would spend my first few days. It was lovely. It had the best pool yet and there was even aquafit equipment that I could use. For two days, I spent a lot of time working out in the pool and taking long walks through the village. I immediately loved it. The village shops closed at lunchtime and the atmosphere was amazingly relaxed. I was delighted to stumble upon a swimsuit shop. I had realized that the swimsuit I brought with me was becoming literally see-through from behind. I had no idea. Might be what attracted the "colleague!" The woman who owned the shop did not speak English. I pointed to the suits and said "Just looking for a new swimsuit." She grabbed her cell phone and called somebody and then handed the phone to me and said "For you." Very confused, I took the phone and said "Hallo," and a man with a strong German accent said "I am the friend of the shop owner, how can we help you?" *How lovely was that!* I told him what I was looking for and he spoke with his friend and translated. This was just the beginning of Bavaria capturing my soul.

I discovered that I was in the heart of the Allgäu region of Bavaria. It is a mountainous region in Southern Germany known for its castles. I was about seventy kilometers north of the German-Austrian Alps. What a great choice I had made. As I wandered through the village I noticed several signs that read "Kneipp & Thermal Im Allgäu." I had no idea what that meant. I found a bench in the middle of the village surrounded by bronze statues and sat and people watched. The people, both young and old, appeared to be a very active and fit. The village did not appear to be a tourist destination and I was thrilled by that. I saw everything from Buddhist statues to Nordic-walking nuns. Matter of fact, there were lots and lots of nuns at the hotel where I was staying. I was a bit surprised by that. The context gave me flashbacks of one of my favorite adventures decades ago when I dressed up as a nun, flew to Las Vegas, and stayed in a hotel that, unbeknownst to me, was also hosting a convention for nuns. But that is a split-your-gut-laughing story that I'll save for another time. I learned from a hotel employee that this particular hotel used to be a convent and that part of the hotel was still a special place for nuns to stay.

The village was quite enchanting with water wheels, statues, and bronze sculptures at every turn. Flowers graced all of the window sills and there were two small grocery stores, wonderful eclectic shops, fabulous little restaurants, cafes with patios, and really happy people. There was a small outdoor concert venue in the middle of the village with a variety of musical entertainment offered throughout the course of my stay in Bad Wörishofen. I continued to try to figure out what the Kneipp & Thermal Im was all about. One of those signs was placed next to what looked like an above-ground cave that you could sit in on benches. I entered and joined the dozen or so other people sitting on the benches which were located around the interior wall. In the middle there was a floor-to-ceiling structure that appeared to be covered in ice. It was very quiet and chilly. And on display, was a photo of a nun with her index finger pressed on her lips. That likely explains the quietness. The more I explored, the more I found statues and tributes to Sebastian Kneipp. I intended to google this person when I returned to my room. The parks surrounding the village were gorgeous, forested, and filled with trails leading to rose gardens, little lakes, and historical sites. There was a totally different fragrance and feel than the grand parks of Marienbad. That evening, I returned to the hotel in time to hear an older gentleman playing an instrument that I could not identify, and German songs being sung by the employees and patrons. *It was awesomely foreign.*

Early on August 18, I checked in at the front desk of Hotel Tannenbaum. I had signed up for their "all-inclusive, full-board" fitness program. The ladies at the front desk did not speak English. I gave them the German version of my paperwork. A delightful woman said "Oh you in lose-kilo program." I laughed out loud. My room was simple and lovely with an extra-long twin bed, a bathroom with tub and shower, and an outside patio with a shortcut to the outdoor pool. I toured the hotel with my schedule for the day in hand. I was told that I could go Nordic walking that afternoon if I wanted to, but during all other days of my stay I would have to go whether I wanted to or not. It was a really hot day and I almost decided not to go, but at the last minute I had a change of heart. The young woman who had conducted my initial intake evaluation was also leading the Nordic walk. There were four of us going on the walk. The staff gave me my own Nordic-walking poles that I would use for the duration of my stay. Our lovely guide showed me how to fasten the poles to my hands and the correct motion for walking with them. This was only the third time I had ever tried Nordic walking. I'm a huge walker and walking is an all important part of my life. But I had only Nordic walked once in Switzerland with poles and no instruction, and once in Marienbad with little instruction. I was a bit hesitant to use the poles because during my other two experiences they really hurt my neck and shoulders, but I didn't want to be a *weenie* so I just bucked up and went.

The path system blew me away. There were paths in every direction and signs indicating distances to a variety of destinations. Tannenbaum 15 min, Sonnenbuchl 25 min, Schoneschach 25 min, Dirlewang 2 h. These were just a few of dozens. It was absolutely astonishing. All of us walked at our own pace and I found myself walking ahead of our instructor. Big mistake! She could see how I was walking with my poles and stopped me many times and tried to help correct what I was doing. I started walking behind her so I could study her technique. I found it incredibly difficult to get the right movement down. We walked those gorgeous, wooded paths for ninety minutes. I was so glad that I went.

We returned about an hour before dinnertime. In the "lose-kilo" program we ate a special diet for our entire stay. Most people came into the program for one week and I was staying for eighteen days. The server directed me to my table for dinner. There were just four of us, three relatively large men and me. It was awkwardly funny. As I have shared I was carrying an extra ten pounds and that was a brand new experience for me. I was still trying to embrace my wiggly-jiggly muffin-top with grace and held an intention to love it away. Two of the gentlemen spoke a little English. They politely asked me what I was doing in their group and at their table. I told them that I was there to get strong. They seemed mildly amused. The food was delicious.

After dinner I took one more walk through the entire hotel. Up, up, upstairs about four flights from my room were the consultation, fitness, and yoga/exercise rooms. Perfect! They were modern, well-equipped rooms with yoga balls, yoga mats, and very advanced exercise machines. On my schedule it looked like we would start each day with aquafit class, then breakfast, followed by a workout/fitness class, which may be yoga, fat burning, or fascia training, followed by lunch, followed by late afternoon Nordic walking. I was thrilled. The facilities were fantastic. I just hoped that the classes would actually happen and that aquafit would last longer than eighteen minutes. I would find out soon enough. The following day would be my first full-schedule day. I turned in early that evening. In addition to the physical fitness and energy that I hoped to attain, I also wanted to delve back into my deep introspective journey. I had been distracted from that for the twelve days that I spent with Adara and for the five days that I spent in Poland. Both were nice distractions, but nonetheless, distractions. *Guess which one I preferred?*

I laid in bed reflecting on my day. This type of end-of-day reflection had become an essential part of my daily practices for well over a decade. I concluded my ritual with asking for assistance in continuing to expand my awareness, and filled with hope that I would hear answers. Again, the questions beckon, *Who Am I? Why Am I?* What do I want? How may I serve? What is the conversation that I most want to participate in and who can most benefit? I intend to live more purposefully. I want to be in service to others. I don't want to die with my music still inside of me. I was tired of knocking on doors. I know I have contributions to make toward a higher consciousness and I am so damn tired of knocking on the doors of people who are vibrating to a lower frequency, but who are also the hiring decision makers. I simply ached to find my venue, the place to speak, teach, learn, and to grow from and with others.

Why have I always had this fascination with endings and with death? Why do I feel misplaced when the default assumption is to direct me to the areas of palliative care and hospice? What is it that I want to say and what do I have to offer? At times the questions haunt me. I keep looking to the *Universe* and saying, "I am trying here! I could use some explicit signs *Lady*!"

Great spirits have always encountered opposition from mediocre minds.

Albert Einstein

Chapter Fourteen

Sweeping

T he last time that I knocked on a door for an opportunity to create programs designed to talk with ease about death and dying, was on the door of the principals of an assisted-living retirement community. Our discussion had been wonderful. Their minds seemed open and I was offered a position on their Life Enrichment Team. But they didn't want me "To get locked into that role, we have bigger plans for you and we can vet your programs at several of our locations." *Fabulous.* Alas, I was going to have the opportunity to utilize my gifts and to be in service. I had not worked inside the assisted-living, memory care world before and I appreciated the opportunity to create and vet programs more than you can imagine. I still wasn't convinced that talking about death at the end of life was my bag, but I thought that the ability to develop programs for the young care team members, the residents' family members, and for the residents just might fit the bill. And equally compelling to me was the potential opportunity to learn from our aging population, our wisdom keepers. We do not live in a consciousness that appears to value the wisdom of our elders. I want to learn from them. I want to hear their stories. I want to tap their wisdom. I have been a wisdom seeker since I was a small child. Who better to seek with than our elders?

So began my seven-month, in-house position on the Life Enrichment Team. The senior living business is quite interesting. It is a multi-billion dollar industry with some of the lowest wages for staff that I have come across in a professional context. With ten thousand people a day turning sixty-five years old in the United States, savvy investors are adding retirement communities to their investment portfolios. I happened to be at one of the most extravagant communities, which exuded the quality of a five-star resort, had incredible amenities, and a jaw-dropping price tag for residents. I would say that ninety-five percent of the residents would not elect to live in assisted-living, no matter how grand. People want to stay in their homes. So as grand a place as it was, I heard daily comments about wanting to go home. I understood. It would be my preference too.

My days consisted of leading balance-fit classes, yoga classes, news-and-views sessions, Ted Talks, and they let me test a meditation class. I was called in on four occasions to the general manager's office for a continued conversation about the programs that we were going "To vet at this location and then at our other locations." I shared in detail many of the components that I thought would make up wonderful programs. At one point we spoke specifically about Atul Gawande's book titled, *Being Mortal*, which was first published in 2014. It is an excellent book, a surgeon's perspective on how medical professionals have approached end of life and how, often under a mask of benevolence, in many cases have contributed to more suffering at the end of life. It is a great read. Very candid, deeply honest, and extremely helpful for each of us to not only give pause to our wishes, but also to take action, to put our ducks in a row, and to openly share our wishes with loved ones and medical professionals. It is an important piece of end of life awareness and preparation. I shared in those few meetings that I had several copies of the book, I owned the PBS Special DVD, and that I had participated on a few local community panels. The *Powers that Be* affirmed that my experience and knowledge was excellent and that we would meet in January to discuss the timing of implementing my programs. It was now the end of October.

About two months later at one of our morning-huddle meetings the head of marketing announced that she had ordered copies of Being Mortal for all employees, recommended everyone read it, and said that there would also be an evening soon where they would be showing the PBS special in our in-house theater. The general manager turned to me in that meeting with his hands held in the prayer position, bowed to me, and thanked me. I thought this was huge progress and eagerly waited for my involvement. With the exception of seeing the books arrive and distributed to employees, I heard nothing further. It was now January and I checked in to see when our meeting would happen. "Soon."

During January and February two residents died. I got to witness up close and personal how this open-minded, progressive group handled death. When the halls were cleared, death went down the elevator, into the underground parking garage, into the ambulance, and out the parking garage door. The residents were not informed. The care team didn't appear to have support or an opportunity to have conversations about death. At the morning huddle, the death of the resident was mentioned to those staff present. I was shocked and stunned. Of course the residents figured it out quickly and there was a buzz and whisper in the air asking questions about how the person(s) died. And there I was right there fully present with the talent, gifts, education, and desire to make a really positive contribution.

March arrived and "the meeting" had not yet happened. I was starting to see and feel that the core management team was more afraid of me talking about death than anything else. At least I think I was butting up against their fears. I was deeply saddened because I knew the kind and quality of contribution that I could make. I felt silenced and led on. Then one afternoon I saw a flyer outside of the in-house theater announcing the showing of Being Mortal that evening. I was really shocked that nobody had kept me up to speed. I went and asked a few of the in-house organizers for any details.

Who was facilitating? They shared the name of the facilitator and I learned that there would also be a panel. Who was on the panel? They provided no information and did not invite me to be a part of the panel discussion.

The day the PBS Special of *Being Mortal* was shown happened to be a day that I was working until 7:00 p.m., and licking my wounds, I watched and listened as the rest of the afternoon and early evening unfolded. I was in the "social" room about twelve feet away from the theater when people started to arrive. I was informed that it was a marketing event open to the community but that "We don't want residents to know." As people were arriving, I was cleaning up the social room where there had just been a messy activity. I was sweeping the floor and watching people walk into the theater. That moment was one of the most pivotal spiritual moments that I have experienced in the past two decades. I *was sweeping* the floor instead of being a part of something I am called to do and have the education and skill set to do. I looked up at the door closing to the theater and I looked down at the broom and I actually laughed out loud. I acknowledged to God et al. that *"I got your message!"* Four weeks later I gave my notice. That night I began planning this ninety-two-day sojourn.

Several residents, who I had fallen absolutely in love with, asked me why I was leaving. I was open and honest about my interests and the programs that I wanted to create. I had their unanimous support. In the weeks after I left there and before I left on my trip, a few of the residents asked if we could have conversations about death and we did, as friends. One resident even asked me to come in and write her and her husband's obituaries. I was honored. We met several times and I elicited and listened to her stories of a lifetime. I wrote their obituaries and she slipped me a one-hundred dollar bill and told me to start my own little business.

I woke up at the crack of dawn. It took me a few minutes to remember that I was in Bavaria at Hotel Tannenbaum. I meditated and then put on my swimsuit and a nice, fluffy robe and headed down the outside path to the building that housed the indoor pool where aquafit classes were taught. A flash of Żądza, the Mime Instructor, ran through my mind and a big shit-eating grin graced my face. My next thought of course was about massage. Massage is not part of the daily program here but it is an option for an additional cost. It is probably a good thing since I seem to have a little bit of slutty in me that I hadn't truly tapped before this trip. I can tell you that for the rest of my life whenever I have a massage, I *will* remember Poland. I arrived at the pool about twenty minutes before class started and grabbed a couple of noodles and a board to start my own "just-in-case" workout. There were a couple of people already in the pool doing their own thing.

At precisely 8:00 a.m. the instructor appeared with boombox in hand. He plugged it in, the music started, and he instructed us to start jogging in a circle. He was speaking German, but run in a circle is fairly easy to decipher since you get run over pretty quickly if you don't comply. I was starting to develop an ear for some of the German words. I had learned some of the German exercise lingo in Schwabisch Hall during yoga class. I was thrilled to understand any words. I sure wish my German grandparents would have taught me to speak German as a child. Our world becomes increasingly expanded as we learn new languages. I think the United States is the least bilingual or multilingual country I have ever spent time in, and I find that a sad state of affairs indeed. Canada is just a kind-of-sort-of bilingual country. Everybody thinks that my people all speak English and French but it just isn't so.

The class lasted for an hour and was absolutely excellent. I was shocked and delighted. After class I returned to my room, changed clothes, and went upstairs to enjoy breakfast with my three gentlemen friends. The table was beautifully set and a little placard that read "Frau Hawks" was placed above the place-setting where I was to sit. The gentlemen were there and all stood up while I sat down. It was a very sweet touch of chivalry. I learned during breakfast that one of the men was leaving later that day, a second one the next day, and the third one in two days. They were all wrapping up their one-week stays. Breakfast was excellent. I would share with you what it was but I have no idea. There were eggs with vegetables, not an omelet and not a scramble. I can tell you that each meal was specifically prepared with health and well-being in mind. I spent most of the time trying to learn the names of the teas so I could order them. We also learned during breakfast that there would be new people arriving over the next few days. I wondered who they would be and what the adventure would be like. I had gotten used to seeing changing faces since my stays at the various places were typically three weeks. I felt excited about it all. I was feeling especially grateful for the quality of the aquafit class. And I was feeling really great about my choice to leave Poland and to come to Bavaria.

The intake evaluation at Tannenbaum was very comprehensive. We weighed-in and then had a really interesting battery of physiological fitness tests. It was all very impressive. After breakfast I wandered around the grounds of the hotel and took pictures. *Oh my God*, the smell of nature in Bavaria is over-the-top wonderful. Hotel Tannenbaum is situated right at the edge of town and opens to acres of hay fields, big old barns, and miles upon miles of trails. *I was in heaven.*

What a beautiful place to help me remember who I really am. My growing up years were spent riding horses, bucking hay, branding cattle, tearing down barns, building fences, and irrigating fields. I simply adore the smell of hay fields, barns filled with hay, and all of it. The scents of Bavaria were rapture to my senses, filling me with flashbacks of the best and the healthiest aspects of my youth. But in Bavaria it's a deeper, more fragrant, more rock-my-world scent. I wanted to bottle the smell. As I wandered around the grounds, across the street, and down a path, I toyed with the idea of what I would call this scent once I figured out how to package it. "Barn Shit" came to mind and I laughed out loud. Like all of my interests, I suspected that the shelf life would have to be for perpetuity. I used to tell my children when they were small that I wanted to hang my Death and Dying shingle, but I couldn't figure out who would come to talk about it; similar principle for my new

"Barn Shit" aroma. Maybe I could offer a discount to attend my seminars to the people who purchased "Barn Shit." They could receive a twenty-percent discount if they attended my Talk about Death seminars. Good God, who are my parents? What galaxy am I from? *I'm a freak!* But I like it that way. Have I mentioned that I am a permanent resident alien? Fits perfectly doesn't it? My guides and angels figured how to give me a signpost for who I really am in 1966 when my alien card was issued.

At 11:30 a.m. I attended the late morning fitness class. It was an excellent workout led by a well-qualified instructor. She kept repeating something again and again. I, of course, had no idea what she was saying or that she was talking to me. One of the class members informed her that "She speaks English," and the instructor said "Oh danka" and came over and helped me get into the correct yoga position. The whole class burst into laughter. At lunchtime I enjoyed another delicious meal and then had an hour or so before our afternoon Nordic-walking session. I was still in awe at the miles and miles of trails leading in and out of forested areas, across fields, and through remote village streets. I couldn't breathe deeply enough to suck in the delicious fresh air. On our walk, the instructor was again attempting to instruct me in the proper use of the poles. It was still such an awkward motion for me. Think about the position and movement of your arms when power walking. That is how I have always moved my arms. Nordic walking is totally different. You start with your arms down by your sides with poles fastened to your hands, and as you walk you push your arms backward and as the poles touch the ground you release them and move your arms back into the starting position. I was still working against myself and it really caused discomfort in my neck and shoulders. I kept studying the motions of the other walkers. They all appeared to be naturals. Their technique was amazing. I was getting flustered. Why couldn't I get the motion down? The group kept chuckling at me. I asked a couple of people who could understand a little English if they had been Nordic walking all of their lives. The answer was a resounding "No!" Then I had the thought that maybe learning to Nordic walk was the perfect metaphor for my life at the moment. I was on a sojourn to examine my story and my life in an attempt to stop the excruciating pain that I had been inflicting on myself, so learning to walk all over again felt appropriate in some ways. Eventually, I figured out how to use the poles correctly and it was extraordinary. No more self-inflicted pain and I felt new strength after each walk.

Before dinner I retreated to my room for some quiet meditation time. A smile beamed through my entire Being. I hadn't felt this free in years. I also had an inner knowing that I had chosen the perfect place for phase three of my grand plan. As I was finishing my thirty-minute meditation, I heard cattle braying loudly. It was music to my ears and I again had flashbacks of my youth. I put on my shoes, grabbed my camera, and shot out the door to a path leading in the direction of the braying. I looked at my watch, it was just about 5:00 p.m., and I deduced that it must be feeding time. I hadn't yet walked in the direction of the huge barn beyond the hay field that bordered Hotel Tannenbaum's property. As I got closer to the barn I could feel an excitement and an aliveness flowing through me. I was flooded with memories of feeding our own horses and cattle. In my early teen years, I used to scramble up the huge stack of hay in our barn and push bales from the top layer and watch them tumble to the ground. We had this amazing barn with three large horse stalls on either side and hay that was stacked fifteen bales high, fifteen bales across, and about twenty bales deep in the middle of the barn. I was often out in the barn feeding on my own and not getting trampled was quite an art form. I learned quickly to toss sections of hay off to the left and off to the right, and let the horses and cattle duke it out while I filled the troughs with hay. Then I would crawl back up on the stack of hay, with my own piece of hay for chew, and watch them feed. *Life was good!* I had a difficult time waiting long enough for my horse's food to digest before hopping on his back, with no saddle and just a hackamore, and riding like the wind. I was so free and alive. I would let him run as fast as he could and feel the sheer power and strength of his muscles envelope me. In the evening with the flood lights on the pasture, the flies around the horses would attract the barn bats. I made it my personal goal while riding to outrun them. I felt lucky and alive. My sisters didn't take to farm life as much as I did. I loved it all, even mucking out the stalls.

The braying sound led me down the Nordic-walking path to an enormous barn which sat at the far edge of the hay field. There was a long rope stretched across the driveway. A farmer driving a red tractor was just coming around the corner of the barn and I waved to him, held up my camera, shrugged my shoulders, and pointed to the cattle. He gave me an affirmative nod and I stepped over the rope. He got off the tractor and went to the left where the calves were contained in a row of open mini stalls separated from the barn. I had never seen anything like them. The back portion was constructed of a heavy white durable plastic. They were dome-shaped, lined with straw, and had a large opening in the front. The front portion of the stall consisted of an enclosure made out of steel poles and rails about four-feet-long, three-feet-wide, and was attached to the enclosed dome. On front of the stalls were round metal holders for huge water pales and huge buckets of milk equipped with long rubber nipples. The calves were all sucking diligently on the nipples. The farmer smiled and then left on his tractor. After photographing the calves, I turned and crossed to the other side of the driveway where all of the moms were feeding in the barn. It was the most magnificent barn I had ever seen. The middle doors were open and in the center of the barn there were seven sections on each side, housing fourteen cattle per side, all facing toward the center where there were enjoying twenty-eight piles of fresh-cut green hay. Each cow wore a leather or metal tubular collar with a chain at the base of her neck and was locked into the feeder. *I felt like I had died and gone to heaven.* I couldn't breathe deeply enough to intake the smell of hay, cattle, milk, and the aging wood of the barn. *My soul smile has been born again.* I took dozens of pictures and stayed until I had to return for dinner.

Each morning there would be a new schedule for the day outside my hotel room door. On the front page it read "Personal Daily Mail, Mrs. Cait Hawks" followed by the date, some lovely photos and an inspirational quote. Today's was "The world is a book and those who do not travel read only a page," by Saint Augustine. On the inside left panel was the day's program with the schedule outlining the times for meals and classes, and on the right panel was the breakfast, lunch, and dinner menu. They even personalized mine in English. It was an extremely impressive program. The morning aquafit and afternoon Nordic-walking classes were constant each day, but the late-morning exercise classes varied each day. I found myself so grateful that I had made the choice to come to Hotel Tannenbaum. I was feeling mentally, emotionally, physically, and spiritually stronger every day.

The program was also beautifully designed to allow for personal downtime, which I found to be perfect for my continued journey to *awarefulness*. It was during these contemplative moments that I continued to try to figure out what called me to death and dying. What was in me or streaming through me that ached to come out? What are my unique gifts and contributions to the service of others? It is not the end of life that most intrigues me, although that is a piece of it. It is more the little deaths along the way that have the potential to prepare us for the end of life that capture my undivided attention. Why do the little deaths hold so much intrigue for me? What is their greater purpose? What can I name them? *I had an aha moment!* For me the little deaths are ego deaths and I believe that they are a very important part of life, specifically designed to prepare us for our actual end-of-life physical death. I will grapple with this later.

I felt very excited to go to dinner that night. Two of the gentlemen in our group had left and I heard that new people were joining the lose-kilo program. I was the first to arrive at our assigned table in the dining room and took a quick glance around at the name placards. I was excited to see that there were two other "Fraus." Not that I didn't enjoy the men, I was simply excited. Franz was the only man left from our original four. He was kind and also spoke a little English. He was still helping me learn the names of the teas. A few of his "hateful" ones became my favorites. The new additions to our lose-kilo group seemed lovely. Both women were German and one spoke decent English. I was trying so hard to learn more German but it was a conversational context and I didn't want to constantly interrupt the getting-to-know each other process. I would recognize a word here and there and over the next few days I understood which teas they were ordering. Hannah, who spoke some English, was thoughtful enough to take a minute during the lively conversations and laughter to lean over and tell me the gist of what was being said. Lebhaft, an incredibly spirited woman who spoke no English, would tell a story or a joke that had everyone just buckling at the knees. They must have been my kind of smutty over-the-top jokes because nobody wanted to translate for me. I wish they would have. I was feeling that Lebhaft and I were kindred spirits. She was a spitfire and I really liked her a lot. She kept everyone laughing to tears during the late morning workouts. I laughed too but didn't have a clue what she was saying. It was just infectious happiness.

The next day on our Nordic walk there was a buzz in the air that two new people would be joining us. We heard that it was a man and a woman. Actually, that's all I heard and understood. I think the rest of the team had more details. At dinner that evening Tolle and Dorothy joined us. They were also German and both very animated and talkative. Franz had one more day in the program. So we had two men and four women in the lose-kilo program that evening. *Whoops*! We had another fabulous lady from Germany join us. I was surprised by the addition of another woman, but nobody else was. It took the rest of us a few days to figure out that Tolle and Dorothy were not married. We had made that assumption because they arrived together, sat next to each other, and bantered like they had known each other their whole lives. We were wrong. Tolle lived in Munich and Dorothy in a small town about an hour away from Munich. We all hit it off wonderfully. *I think.*

On Tolle's second day in the program, he suggested to the rest of us that we move aquafit classes to the outside pool instead of the smaller inside pool. I told him that it was a great idea but that it would be way too cold for me. He assured me that it wasn't, but I was not a believer. The rest of the team squelched the idea almost immediately. That night at dinner Tolle made the proposal again to move the class outside. He said that if I paid attention in the morning, I would see steam coming off the pool, and that "It is because it is heated." The next morning I started down the path from my room to the neighboring building with the indoor pool, but stopped, turned around, and went and dipped my toe in the gorgeous outdoor pool. *It was not very cold!* I stepped into the outdoor shower and then gritted my teeth as I walked down the steps into the shallow end of the pool. The slight chill took my breath away for about thirty seconds and then it was absolutely tremendous. *A believer was born!* From that moment on, Tolle and I spent each morning facilitating our own outdoor aquafit classes. We would go to the indoor pool before class started and gather our noodles and foam boards and return to the outside pool. Try as we might to convince the others to at least try it, nobody did.

Tolle and I took our combined knowledge of the exercises and created many of our own. We ached from laughter and fully immersed ourselves in that magical, pristine environment. Each morning the steam off the water enveloped us as the sun rose enough to cast its light on the east end of the pool. The pool was situated right next to the hay field. It was the most blissfully-pure fragrant air that I have ever breathed. The pool was surrounded with white lounge chairs and umbrellas and there was a white marble statue of a woman pulling her pony tails at the east end. *It was spectacularly delicious, scrumptious, and over-the-moon soulful.* My stay at Tannenbaum would be a week longer than Tolle's and I wondered who would arrive in the program that I could talk into joining me every morning. In the meantime, I was in a state of pure bliss.

Goodbyes are only for those who love with their eyes. Because for those who love with heart and soul there is no such thing as separation.

Rumi

Chapter Fifteen

Emotional Goodbyes

By the end of the first week I was starting to remember who I am at a cellular level. Laughter from the pit of my Being was spilling out of me. I was remembering what it felt like to be joyous, filled with bliss, and grounded.

The fitness program was exceptional. The classes, in addition to daily morning aquafit and afternoon Nordic walking, were one (or two) of the following: power yoga, fat burner, bellies-legs-and-bottom, fascia training, and training of the pelvic-floor muscles and abdominal workout. The instructors were excellent and we laughed a lot and sweated bullets. I couldn't understand a word of the instruction but that cued the instructors to pay special attention to me; which, at times, I would have rather hidden in a back corner of the room in my pool of sweat. But nope, they had me front and center. Lebhaft, of course, was in the back of the room telling her jokes that kept everyone in stitches. At the end of the week everybody except me was thrilled that they had survived. I had another week of the classes after they left. At the end of the week we also had another fitness consultation and weigh-in. It was a remarkably top-notch program.

On several of our Nordic-walking outings, we came across areas tucked in the woods that contained wooden benches bordering a concrete, rectangular pool about ten-feet long, fifteen-feet wide, and eighteen-inches deep, with steps and handrails that led down into freezing cold water. There were also concrete troughs situated at a distance from the pool. They were about waist-high and filled with ice cold water. We were instructed to either step into the pool of water, walk slowly, and with each step lift our foot up out of the water and then back in, or to go to the trough of ice water and immerse an arm up to the shoulder, hold the position for thirty seconds to one minute, and then repeat with the other arm and shoulder. I felt spectacular after walking in the pools and after immersing my arms in the troughs. There was signage indicating that these were Kneipp healing areas.

The head of the fitness program, who spoke decent English, shared with me that Kneipp healing treatments were founded by a priest named Sebastian Kneipp, and that he was one of the forefathers of naturopathic healing. These pools and troughs were built as a form of hydrotherapy treatment. In the mid 1800's, Kneipp had built several hospitals in Bad Wörishofen. The Tannenbaum fitness program was modeled after his beliefs. This is another attestation to the health and well-being of the people of Bavaria. I finally understood why there were so many statues paying tribute to Sebastian Kneipp in the village and the parks. They also hold a Kneipp Anniversary Festival every year. I enjoyed a day at his anniversary festival during my stay. I couldn't have landed in a better place for this phase of my journey.

We experienced all sorts of weather in Bavaria. Some days were spanking hot, others were drizzling with light rain, and we were even blessed with two evenings of the best thunder and lightning storms I have ever witnessed. I adore thunder and lightning. We don't get too many of those in the Pacific Northwest. By the end of week one I had added walks to the village, which was only two kilometers away, to my daily routine. Again, I found myself adoring spending weeks in one place. I would stop in the shops and say

"Hallo" to the shopkeepers that I was getting to know. One of the Nordic-walking nuns had even taken to making eye contact with me and giving me a little wave. I felt grateful that she had no knowledge of me having been excommunicated from the Catholic Church at age six! If the shops were closed for their midday break I would walk through the parks surrounding the village.

On one particular day while strolling through the parks, I came across an in-ground trough that was filled with brick-red colored mud. A woman had her pants rolled up over her knees and was walking back and forth. There was signage describing the health benefits but of course I couldn't read the German. It was clear though that walking in the red mud was for its health benefits. As I continued my walk, I came across families with small children who were all barefoot and walking on a large circle of oblong-shaped pine cones. There was a large white sign to the left of the pine cones, and on it, a depiction of the sole of a large foot with a circle of pine cones underneath the arch of the foot. The sign read Zapfen-Fuss with two paragraphs of text underneath. It appeared to me to be a form of natural reflexology therapy. All contributions, I believe, as to why the people of Bavaria appeared to be so healthy, happy, and content.

Żądza and I had been in contact since I left Poland. On a couple of occasions he said, "I invite you to come back to Poland," but I shared with him that I was very happy to be in Bavaria and that the program I was in was just perfect for me. I invited him to come and visit me there. I was quite surprised when he said yes. He was going to plan a trip to come for my last few days in Bavaria. I found myself extremely delighted and very excited that he would make the two-flight, three-train journey. *Mother Teresa seems to like me!* He was so perfectly placed on my path. After my experience with the galloping man, I had found myself feeling so beat up. And at times, as women, I think it's easy to fall into the trap of feeling unattractive and undesirable. I had. Apparently, Mother Teresa and my angels had conspired and arranged for the perfect, hot, younger, gifted, handsome man to cross my path at exactly the right moment to remind me that not only was I attractive, but also to wake-up that sensual side of me again. I sported a huge grin on my face just thinking about his arrival the following week.

The day before several of our group members were scheduled to leave the program, Tolle asked me if I would like him to take me to Neuschwanstein Castle in the Alps. He shared that he had time that Saturday morning, that it was only seventy kilometers away, and that he would love to take me. I responded with a resounding *yes!* I had learned that Neuschwanstein Castle was built by King Ludwig II in 1869, as a place for the shy king to retreat from the public. It is one of the most famous castles in the whole of Europe and it is the castle that Walt Disney designed the Cinderella Castle after. On Saturday, Tolle and I drove to the castle. The drive was spectacularly beautiful, with windy country roads, little German villages, shockingly green hillsides and forests, and an occasional pristine lake with the majestic Alps looming in the background. The closer we got, the louder I could feel my heart beating with excitement.

When we arrived we parked the car in a lot at the base of the mountain. We discussed our options for getting up to the castle. Neuschwanstein Castle was an obvious tourist destination. There were crowds of people everywhere. We had the options of walking up the road to the castle, taking a bus, or riding in a horse-drawn carriage. Being the fit and strong people who we had become, we chose the horse-drawn carriage. The wait in line was a bit long but the ride up was just outstanding. Once we arrived at the castle we had a choice of paying to tour the inside, much of which was under renovation, but we elected not to go inside. We opted to stay outside and suck it all in. There were hang gliders flying above the castle and views to die for. *I don't have words to describe the magic that I felt.* In the distance we could see a bridge stretching from one peak to another with lots of people maneuvering their way across it. I don't have a clue how they built it or when it was built but I have got to tell you that I don't think, with my fear of heights, that I could have mustered the courage to walk across it. It gave me flashbacks of a swinging bridge at the Calgary zoo that my father took us across when we were small children. It was terrifying. And this bridge was much higher and plummeting down to the rocky terrain and waterfall below looked like a way that I did not want to exit planet earth.

Tolle and I drove back in the late afternoon. He is such a delightful human being. I've given him the name Tolle in the book because Tolle is the German word for "amazing." On the drive back he shared with me that just over a decade ago he had worked for a company that sent him to the United States to work for a couple of years. He said that he was based in California but spent Monday through Friday in the greater Seattle area. I was stunned and asked which company. He said that I would never know the company or the city. I asked him to give me a shot. He told me the company name and I asked "At their location in Issaquah?" He looked at me absolutely shocked and said "How is it possible that you could know that?" I shared with Tolle that I lived in Issaquah from 1984 through 2005, that I raised my children there, and that I watched them build the building where he worked. We started tracing back the dates that he was there. At the time he was in Issaquah, I lived about a mile away and we figured out that we shopped at the same stores, went to the same bookstore, and saw movies at the same theater. We were both gobsmacked, as my British friends would say. We surmised that we had to have crossed paths on a regular basis. Then Tolle said, "You know I booked this week at Hotel Tannenbaum and then on my way here I decided to change my mind because it wouldn't feel like a vacation being only eighty kilometers from my home in Munich, but then I had this feeling to turn the car around and come anyway." We were both taken aback by the synchronicities of the *Universe,* and how after so many potential opportunities to meet, that we would end up meeting in Bavaria twelve years later. It was a moment of affirmation that I was exactly where I was supposed to be; *magical moments indeed!*

It was hard to say goodbye to the people in our group that were leaving. Tolle, Dorothy, Hannah, and Jenna all departed. It was the end of their stay in the lose-kilo program. Only Lebhaft and I remained. She would also leave in another day or two. I was overwhelmed with emotion saying goodbye to them after such a nourishing week filled with so much laughter, health, and well-being. I worked diligently to learn enough German words to get to know Lebhaft a little better. I knew I adored her, I just couldn't understand what she was saying and I desperately wanted to. I wanted to tap her humor because I knew that her stories and jokes would be ones that I would enjoy sharing for years to come. I did learn that she had no children, had never married, and was quite happy about that.

The next day a husband and wife (who spoke too much English) and another gentleman, all from Germany, joined our group. I found myself feeling sad at dinner that evening. I missed the dynamic and the closeness that I had felt with our regular team. I continued to do aquafit in the outside pool, and as much as I tried to convince the others that it was the most magical experience, nobody joined me. I missed Tolle. I missed them all, but was also grateful to have another week in the program and immersed with the people of Bavaria. Plus, Żądza would be coming in a few days. I reflected on the "special" massages and my sadness quickly passed. I enjoyed Żądza so much in Poland and how we had ached from laughter. Mostly, I was laughing at him. He spoke such broken English, and he did not have prepositions down *at all,* which made the things he said absolutely hysterical. Thank goodness that one of his gifts was to belly laugh at himself. *At least I think he was laughing at himself.*

Over the next several days I took long evening walks on the Nordic trails by myself and would choose one of the dozens of benches to sit on and reflect. Germany and the German people are so impressive and build things so mindfully. All of the benches have metal placards on them with an identifying number so if anyone should need emergency help, they can call and give the bench number and be found quickly. My thoughts were focused on my deep driving desire to serve, my professional direction, and continuing to listen deeply to what called me to these ego deaths, as I refer to them.

> When you are whole you are holy and you are
> healed. When you are whole you also lose the
> fear of death because you realize death is a
> creative opportunity to recreate yourself.

Deepak Chopra

Chapter Sixteen

What is this Thing Called Death?

I think that all fear is a fear of death but not just the end-of-life death of the physical body. I contemplated the larger context of death. The death of a belief system. The death of a relationship. The death of an identity. The death of the many roles that we play and so strongly identify with. The death of a story we have been living. I began to reflect on the many ego deaths that I have experienced. We all experience so many of these deaths, and I see the potentiality they hold to truly prepare us for our exit out of this physical body. That is, of course, assuming that we are even in our physical body.

Over the years as I have been knocking on doors and seeking my venue with like-minded people, I have heard repeated requests that we not call death "Death." Most of them say things like "Do we have to call it death? Can't we call it something else?" I have always been struck by that. Why would we want to call death by another name when the potential exists for us to overcome our fears, to find peace, and to understand *who and why we really are*? It is only the ego that shudders at the possibility of death. Now why on earth, since we are all going to shed this physical body, do we not want to choose to prepare to die with as much grace and understanding as possible, and to call death by its name? As I returned to my room still pondering this question, I hopped online and looked up the definition of death.

> Wikipedia defines death this way: "Death is the cessation of all biological functions that sustain a living organism. Phenomena which commonly bring about death include aging, predation, malnutrition, disease, suicide, homicide, starvation, dehydration, and accidents or trauma resulting in terminal injury. In most cases, bodies of living organisms begin to decompose shortly after death.

> Oxford Dictionary defines death as: "The action or fact of dying or being killed; the end of the life of a person or organism."

> Merriam Webster Dictionary reads: Definition of death for English Language Learners: the end of life. The time when someone or something dies. The ending of a particular person's life. The permanent end of something that is not alive. The ruin or destruction of something.

After reading a dozen or so definitions of the word death I started to develop more of an appreciation for the desire of others to call death by another name. The current definitions are so morbid and reek of such finality. My heart calls me to engage in dialogues with others for the purpose of calling into question our beliefs about death, and to bring to our awareness where our beliefs come from. And then to facilitate, and engage in, conversations where we remain curiously open for the purpose of collaborating in elevating the current consciousness. I find it important to call death, death.

I believe that the question *"Who Am I?"* can only be fully explored by looking at death, talking about death, and examining the ego deaths that we are each blessed to experience. What is death? What dies? Why is this subject so ominous and riddled with fear?

Let me start by sharing my experience with obvious deaths, the deaths of physical bodies; the deaths of people that have touched my life. This might sound weird but I have been blessed with saying goodbye to so many people I have loved. The first person that I have a memory of dying was a great aunt. I was four years old and asked to go wake-up my aunt from a nap. She wouldn't wake-up. She had died peacefully in her sleep. My great uncle broke down in tears. Over the next day or so I remember sitting and watching each family member's reaction to my aunt's death. Some people were crying, some were talking and visiting. I remember my aunt's body being laid out in the living room on some kind of table or something. I vividly remember touching her with a childlike curiosity. I wasn't afraid, I was much more fascinated.

Later, during my teenage years my favorite aunt died, she was in her forties. My best friend's brother died, he was eighteen. And a very special lady who had a profound influence on my life died, she was in her forties. I remember taking long walks in the evening and pondering death. What was it? Why did I still feel very connected to these people? In my twenties my grandfather and my grandmother died. And in my thirties my father (the man who raised me), and my first love and very dear friend died. In my late forties and early fifties, my sister died, three very dear friends died, my first husband died, and most recently my second husband died. All of these deaths certainly affected me. They affected me deeply and my questioning about death deepened.

I think the deaths though, that really dropped me to my knees, were the deaths of Dr. David Simon and Dr. Wayne Dyer. They are two of my greatest mentors and have had such a profound effect on my life. The blessing however, is that I can still pick up their books and read their wisdom, and I can listen to their voices on their CD's and watch them on their DVD programs. What a gift that is. *What an incredible gift!* I think we should all take heed and leave similar gifts for the ones that we love. I really mean that and can't recommend it strongly enough. With all of the technology available at our fingertips, we should give long and considerable thought to leaving our own audio and video messages as part of our legacy, for our loved ones.

With my farm upbringing I also experienced death on a regular basis. I witnessed the birth of still-born calves, and horses that had to be put down. We also raised rabbits and there were dozens and dozens of baby rabbits that the moms either pushed out of the nest, or ate half of their little bodies. I remember one night in particular when I was in high school and was getting ready to go to the movies with my best friend, but I had to feed the rabbits first. It was a very cold, snowy Idaho night. As I was feeding the rabbits I noticed a frozen new baby under the cage. I gathered it up in my hands and was running to put its little body in the trash when it started moving. The warmth of my hands had brought the little bunny back to life, so I took it inside the house, put it on a heating pad, and went with my friend to the movies. When we returned the poor little thing was boiling. I had set the heat on the pad too high. Death by freezing would have been a much kinder passing. *Poor little rabbit.* We also raised a calf every year or so and would butcher it and fill our freezer. And there were barn cats and kittens that died, and snakes that got caught in the hay bailer. It was the natural cycle of life and death, except for that baby rabbit. I am so grateful for those experiences. I know many, many people my age who have never seen death up close and personal, and as such, I think their first experiences of loss are met with such unpreparedness.

In generations past, death was much more up close and personal. Today death seems more removed, more hidden, more laden with fear, and more unexpected. It has always taken me aback a bit when an elder very late in life dies and so many people state that "It was so unexpected." I have often thought "How can it be so unexpected, they were in their nineties?" I respect the meaning behind their comments and I also find it a bit naïve. I feel that the combination of fear and denial is a very difficult way to approach death. I want to participate in conversations about death and dying. I want to help people explore their own thoughts about death, and also to explore where those beliefs came from. I don't necessarily want people to believe what I believe. My beliefs come from my lived experience and how thoughts and ideas surrounding death resonate with my lived experience. My beliefs are also deepened by my spiritual practices. I would really like to help people engage in these most important conversations, and encourage them to remain curiously open to new thoughts and ideas that they may have never before pondered. I think that Deepak Chopra's comment that "Death is a creative opportunity to recreate yourself," is one of the most delicious ways to think about death. I believe that death is our birthright. And that the moment we die was written into our grand design from the moment that we took our first breath. How we reach that moment is filled with a lifetime of our own choices and free will.

So the questions I put forth are, "When we die, what dies? Who dies?" I personally believe that all death is the death of the Ego. It is with this understanding that I am drawn to the little ego deaths along the way that I believe are rich with potentiality to prepare us for the ultimate death of our physical body. Let me provide some examples from my own life of what ego deaths mean to me.

My first experience of an ego death happened when my parents divorced when I was four years old. It was the death of a relationship as I knew it. My father, who I loved dearly, was no longer present in my daily life. And as the years passed I rarely saw him. I digested that experience internally and I was a sickly little child with ulcers. What was the ego death? I was no longer a little girl with the presence of my father. There was no longer our father-daughter relationship as I had known it. It was a death of knowing *who I am* in that relationship.

The next ego death, which had a huge impact on me, occurred when I was ten years old. I had been raised in a Catholic family and had attended Catholic Church. Even though I was not baptized Catholic, I still attended the sermons and Sunday school. I was still exposed to and learning the belief system. Then I went to my friend's Mormon Church with her and I was hearing a different set of beliefs. It shook me to my core. I ran out of the church and around to the side garden and cried. I just didn't know what to believe and I wanted to believe *the Truth*! That was another ego death. The death of a belief system that was meaningful to me and it *rocked my world*. A death of what I believed about *the Truth* existing.

Then there was the death of the relationship with my first love and best friend. We were twenty-one years old. He was in a terrible car accident and was left with a severe head injury and brain trauma. He didn't physically die until many years later but it was the death of our relationship as I knew it. It was such a tough experience to be the only one of the two of us who still held the memories we once shared. It was a death of I am this to you and you are this to me. It was the death of a shared first love, the death of a friendship made more challenging because he was still alive but with no memories of us. I have often felt that people who have a family member living through the stages of dementia must feel this same way. It is an experience of death long before our loved one dies. Without a context to openly engage in a dialogue about this kind of ego death makes the experience extremely agonizing.

During my twenties, I was pursuing my undergraduate education and my goal was to go to law school. I had married young and had given birth to my daughter just twelve months later, so I was pursuing my education on the much harder path of working full time, being a mom, and going to evening classes. It ultimately took me eleven years to complete a bachelor's and a master's degree. Upon completing my bachelor's degree and having been accepted into law school, I did a one-hundred-and-eighty-degree turn and decided to pursue a master's degree instead. That too, was an ego death. It was the death of an ideal and a vision that I had held tightly to. I identified so strongly with the academic path I was on and all of the ego associations with one day becoming a lawyer. After all of those years of justifying my commitment to my education, it was very unnerving to just simply and radically change direction. I remember the day that I was telling my husband, a lawyer, that I had decided not to pursue law school. I felt like a sixteen-year-old girl who was telling her father that she was pregnant. It was a time of a total redefinition of who I am, and it was the death of a story that I had been telling myself and the world. Now who was I?

I have mentioned how difficult the deaths of Dr. Wayne Dyer and Dr. David Simon were for me. Those too were ego deaths. These were two of my greatest teachers and I was a devoted student of the work and their teachings. In a sense, I now felt that they were no longer my teachers and I was no longer their student. Except for the blessing of the works they left behind. Part of what I valued so much was their own paths of consciously evolving and how their teachings evolved. I feared that without them my own conscious evolution might be hindered. That was a terrifying feeling to me.

There have also been numerous ego deaths in the changing and redefining of roles that I have played as a wife, as a mother, as a partner, as a sister, as an aunt, as a teacher, as an employee, and as a friend. Each of our lives is permeated with ego deaths that are rich with potentiality to better understand *who we really are*. Reflect for a moment on your own life and see if you can trace back your own little ego deaths. Perhaps it will help for me to clarify that ego to me is our identification with *I Am This* and *I Am That*. I am a mother, I am a teacher, I am a sister, I am a daughter, I am five-foot, eight-inches tall, I am single, I am divorced, I am gainfully employed, I am independent. I am. I am. I am. What I am proposing is that we each take into consideration the life-giving opportunity to pay thoughtful attention to the roles we play, the transitions we go through, the angst that we feel, and to use these experiences to explore and understand *who we really are.*

I have shared with you that Jet and I handled divorce better than most couples I've ever known. It was a long and arduous process for me to identify as Jet's friend and not his wife and partner. Jet and I did an excellent job of never defining him as stepfather and we never considered our children as half brother and sister. I was their mother, simple as that. He was their father. However, when Jet died, when he actually shed his physical body, I began my role as Executor/Trustee. We had defined our family as family, plain and simple. Now the legal and business world that I have been immersed in while handling the business of death has defined me and my family in ways that we never did. It has been a real ass-kicking.

These new definitions of me and our family started with the writing of Jet's Will. The lawyer said "OK so you have one child," and Jet said "No, I have two children." The lawyer replied "But you only have one legal, natural child and one stepchild." Jet was incredibly upset and did not want his Will to read that way and he added an additional clarifying sentence. Since the time of Jet's death, I have been consistently referred to as the "ex-wife," and questioned at each turn along the path as to whether Jet really designated me as his Executor and Trustee. I have one child that exists for legal purposes and another "stepchild" who for all legal intent and purposes has no natural rights to things left behind. This process of redefining me and my children by the larger consciousness has been going on for what feels like an eternity and it sucks. It is death plus death, little ego deaths at every turn. Wayne Dyer's words that "Other people's opinions of me are none of my business" help to bring me back to center.

All week I spent my evening time on those simple benches on the Nordic-walking paths of Bavaria, deeply examining the *I Am's* that I have so strongly identified with, and how those ego identifications have shaped my story; both the story that I have been telling myself and the story that I have been sharing with the world. It's all pretty screw bally when you really think about life this way. *Who Am I really?*

We're wired for sensual pleasure from the start. Our physical bodies were formed through sex. Human life itself is, in fact, sexually transmitted.

Christiane Northrup

Chapter Seventeen

Guess Who's Coming to Bavaria?

Żądza would be arriving in two days and I found myself extremely excited to see him. We had plans to go to the Alps and cross over into Austria. I had been looking at routes and hotel rooms and had reserved a car. In the meantime, the fitness program at Tannenbaum continued to be excellent. I was feeling very strong, deeply nourished, and really happy. The days were passing far too quickly. It was the end of August already and I would leave Bavaria on September 5, travel back to London, spend a few days with my dear friends, and fly home on September 9. I couldn't believe that it was almost the end of my ninety-two days. I had thought that I might get homesick because I had never been away for such an extended period of time. But I was not even remotely feeling homesick. I was not ready to go back to life as I knew it. Ah, but then I reminded myself that life won't be as I have known it because I was examining my story. I was embracing and healing the shadow aspects of myself. I was preparing to live a happier story, and to invite nice and kind into my life where there had been an absence of those qualities in others that I had too frequently allowed into my world. I was expanding my awareness. I was in the process of realizing a story of an easier life, a more fulfilled life, a nourishing life, a shared life, with the opportunity to not die with my music inside of me. *That excited the pants off of me, either that or the man that was heading my way.*

On September 1, I woke up filled with exhilaration. Żądza was arriving late that night. I was in the outdoor pool at the crack of dawn and wondering why I felt such excitement to see him. He was lovely, he was kind, he was tall and handsome, and he thought that I have a "supaw bottom." Yes, that was the totally physical part of the attraction and the excitement. Deeper than that though was what he woke up in me. I felt attractive and alive with Żądza. He had awakened my sensual sleeping Goddess and wide awake that Goddess was. Did I hope that this relationship would become more? Nope, I really didn't and I don't think he did either. I loved the adventure of it all, and I absolutely adored the simple pleasures and the outrageous laughter. There was innocence and simplicity to this man that I thoroughly loved. Who he is was right out there in the open. But I did not see the situation as a life partner love story. It just was what it was. *Thank you Mother Teresa!*

A storm had moved in the day before Żądza's arrival and I heard that the news was reporting possible flooding in the Allgäu, including along the route that we would take to the Alps. I wasn't even considering changing our plans, until the third lovely hotel employee knocked on my door and said that I should not plan to drive to the Alps. I remained open to the possibility that the storm would pass.

I walked in the pouring rain to the village late that evening. I had previously confirmed with a pizza restaurant that they would be open until 10:00 p.m. Żądza would arrive just after 11:00 p.m. When I had spoken to him last, he told me that he liked pizza and I was certain he would be starving after his two-airplane, three-train trip. I arrived at the restaurant at 9:00 p.m. It was the first time that I had walked late at night to the village. It was twinkling with lights, and just dazzling. I enjoyed a glass of wine and waited for the pizza. With the few German words that I spoke, I shared with the owner that I had a friend arriving on the late train. He told me to stay inside until they were ready to close and leave; *lovely people*. At 10:30 p.m. I took the pizza and walked the remaining two blocks to the train station, which wasn't really much of a station. I had checked it out a few days prior so that I knew what I was in store for. There was no place to wait inside, just an outside covered platform and a modest bench. After about a thirty-minute wait on the bench, the train arrived and I could see Żądza in the first car with a beaming smile and waving madly. I laughed out loud wondering if it was me or the pizza box that got him so excited.

It was midnight by the time we arrived at Tannenbaum. We had eaten the pizza while walking in the pouring rain. It was spectacular. When we got to my room, Żądza suggested that we "Exercise in bed, then sleep." Oh my God there's that crazy laughter again. I said "Why not Babe!" He responded "No Caiti, I Żądza." I didn't even try to contain the laughter. He laughed too but I'm not sure why. The thunder and lightning storms throughout the night contributed to making that night a particularly wonderful memory. I had been a bit concerned about sharing my twin-sized bed, until I remembered that it was actually twice the size of the massage table.

The next morning I went to the front desk to get directions to walk to the rental car facility. I hadn't been able to find it earlier in the week but I knew it was located within blocks of the train station. The front desk people told me not to rent the car. They insisted it was a bad idea. I asked Żądza, and he agreed. They called and cancelled the car for me. Even after having given pause to my plans from their earlier warnings, I had remained hopeful to make our trip to the Alps. I was really bummed. I had found this lovely little hotel in Austria not far from the German border, but I was also not foolish enough to not heed the advice of the local people.

Żądza gave me a huge hug, and suggested that instead, we take the train to Munich and spend the day "With beer." I burst into laughter and agreed.

At the train station we could not figure out how to get our tickets from the machine. Of course the instructions were all written in German. A lovely young lady who worked at Tannenbaum happened to walk by and see our dilemma. She gave us a quick lesson, and *walah*, we had our round-trip tickets. We would need to make two train changes, and Żądza assured me that he knew exactly the stops to make the changes since he had just done it last evening. He had the train route maps and he said "Caiti, you trust me, I know way." We boarded, found our seats, and set our dripping wet umbrellas aside. He showed me the map and said, "Five stops then we change." I was looking at the map and felt grateful that he had just done the trip, because from my reading we would change trains at the first stop. I was confused. Just then a woman came through the cars checking tickets. I asked her at which stop we would change trains for "Munchen?" She replied "Next stop." Żądza was shocked. Within two minutes we were at the next stop and got off the train. As I walked to the front of the train I busted at the seams in laughter. There was a concrete wall in front of the train where it stopped. I motioned to Żądza to come and see, and pointing to the concrete wall, I said "Trust you?" We laughed until we ached.

We arrived in Munich, left the station, and guessed which direction to walk to the Old Square. As luck would have it we guessed correctly. There were people and umbrellas everywhere. The chapel bells were ringing. It was total awesomeness. The square was loaded with outdoor beer gardens and we sat on a bench in one of the gardens for about ten minutes before the large table umbrella started dumping water on our heads. Drenched and laughing, we ran across the square and found a marvelous indoor restaurant. A waitress, who had overheard me talking, brought me a menu in English. I thanked her but I do prefer the adventure of just pointing to something on the German menu and seeing what

I get. We ordered the Bavarian Peasant's Feast and "tall beers." The description on the menu read "Pickled and roast pork, with roast sausage, served with sauerkraut and white bread dumpling." Talk about veering away from all of the "special" meals that I had been eating in the lose-kilo program.

All of the servers and many of the patrons were dressed in the traditional Bavarian Tracht, women wearing Dirndl and the men sporting Lederhose. We had a fabulous time. And after he had consumed a few beers, Żądza remarked that "Women love me because I so handsome." I was on my game and by now was very certain that his so-called "fluency" in English was rudimentary, at best. So I replied "Well aren't you just a pompous little ass." When his face lit up and he said "Yes Caiti," I laughed so hard that a little beer came out my nose. We enjoyed ourselves there for hours.

Late in the evening we found our way back to the train station and caught our train heading for Bad Wörishofen. The rain had turned to drizzle. Regardless, upon our arrival we chose to take a taxi back to Tannenbaum. It was late and we had bellies full of great food and beer. We slept soundly that night. The next morning the rain had completely stopped and we decided to rent a car and drive to the Alps. We wouldn't have enough time to cross into Austria but at least we had a day to return to those captivating mountains and the absolutely stunning countryside. The general manager of the hotel was kind enough to drive us to the car rental facility. Once we rented the car, Żądza drove and I *kind of sort of* remembered how to point us in the right direction. It was a gorgeous sunny day and the drive was extraordinarily beautiful. I told Żądza about a lake that I had spotted near a little village called Füssen on the way to the Alps when I had gone to the castle with Tolle. When we got to that area he turned down the country dirt road leading to the lake. It was beautiful. We spent some time meandering down to the shore. The lake was riddled with sailboats anchored off shore, and in the distance we could see a forested shoreline behind which were open green meadows leading right up to those ominous mountains. It was just breathtaking. We lingered for an hour while I shot dozens of photos.

We arrived at the same place that Tolle and I had gone the previous Saturday. We opted not to go up to see the castle, the lines were much longer that day and Żądza had also visited Neuschwanstein before. So we continued driving to neighboring villages situated at the base of the Alps. We found a small local restaurant with wooden benches outside and enjoyed lunch, a cold beer, and watched the hang gliders take off from the mountain top in the near distance. I felt so physically, mentally, and spiritually well. I felt nourished. After several hours of exploring it was time to head back. As we neared Füssen, Żądza again turned down the dirt road to the lake. I was delighted. He sat at a table on the outdoor patio near the lake's edge while I darted about taking more photographs. As I was looking through the lens of my camera at the sailboats, the lake, the Alps, and the man at the patio table, I was overwhelmed with a feeling of sadness about leaving Bavaria. This place and her people had touched me at a soul level. I did not want to quit breathing the pristine air, nor did I want to leave the beauty that just rocked my world. We arrived in Bad Wörishofen in the evening and returned the rental car. This time we decided to walk back to Tannenbaum. The next day would be the last day of his visit and my last day in Bavaria too; then we would both be leaving on September 5. He would be taking trains and planes home to Kolobrzeg. And I would be taking the hotel shuttle to Munich for my flight to Heathrow for my final four days of this amazing summer with no story.

We woke the next morning to a gorgeous day. I went upstairs and worked out and then back to our room to get changed into my swimsuit so I could go suck up all of the deliciousness of the pool for one last time. Żądza was already in the pool when I got there. I was really hoping for another mime-led aquafit experience, but instead he just enjoyed the pool. I stayed in the pool for two hours that morning trying to metabolize the experience at every level of my Being, so that I could carry the memories home with me.

I felt that if I could recreate that same experience for the start of everyday for the rest of my life, *then my life just got made!*

After I dragged myself away from the pool, we decided to spend the day walking on the Nordic paths and then through the parks. We would end up in the village where we would have one last dinner together. We walked down the trails to a remote village that had a lookout point to the Alps. On the walk back, I taught Żądza how to moo at the cattle and have them moo back, a very impressive skill that I learned during my growing-up years on the farm. He was shocked. I told him to try it in Polish, and then *peed my pants* laughing. We made our way to the village by dinnertime and enjoyed our last meal together. We arranged a taxi for Żądza for a 5:30 a.m. pick-up the next morning for his early train. I thought about taking the train with him because the Munich airport was the point of departure for both of us, but I elected to take the shuttle from Tannenbaum a few hours later instead. I think I felt it would be easier to say goodbye that way. In the morning the taxi did not show, and my last image of Żądza was of him running like the wind down the street to the train station. It was another quick goodbye.

Two hours later I was in the shuttle with the driver and a lovely woman from New Zealand who had been so kind to me during our stay at Tannenbaum. On several occasions she had played the role of translator for me. She had been coming to Tannenbaum for a month every summer for many years, and was not only a beautiful human Being, but also a wonderful resource. She sat in the front seat with the driver and they enjoyed a long conversation in German all the way to the Munich airport. I sat in the back seat trying to hold back tears until I couldn't hold them back anymore. I am not typically someone who wants to return to the same place again and again because there is so much more of the world to see. But in this instance, I made a vow to myself that I would return to peaceful, beautiful Bavaria and to the people who make her so special.

My flight was not scheduled to depart until 3:00 p.m. so I had about six hours to settle in at the Munich airport, catch my breath, wipe my tears, and start uploading photos to my computer. As I got my wits about me it occurred to me that I still had four days in London to see my dear friends. I hadn't seen George and Olivia for about six years and my excitement started to kick in. I was also hoping to see James one more time while I was in London.

Friends are God's way of apologizing for your family.

Wayne Dyer

Chapter Eighteen

Blessed Friends

It was a quick two-hour flight from Munich to Heathrow. George would be picking me up at the airport and driving me to their home in Wimbledon. As I entered the customs/passport control area I was wishing I was an EU Citizen because that line was only ten people deep. My line, on the other hand, was about one hundred people deep. After about an hour, I made it to the front of the line and breezed through customs. I grabbed my suitcase and paused, did I want to exit through the Nothing To Declare door or Declare Goods door? I giggled to myself because the only thing I had to declare was my freedom. Over the past eighty-eight days I had been rested, nourished, woken up, strengthened, and lubed. I actually felt like I had a lot to declare!

Patiently awaiting me on the other side of the door was my dear, dear George. *Oh my, it is so great to see him.* We embraced, laughed, made each other do a twirl and then headed out to the parking garage. It was about an hour-plus drive to Wimbledon. We chatted and chatted and caught up on life. It kept striking me strange that I could understand everything he was saying. It had been awhile since I was with an English speaker, and proper English at that. Olivia was at home waiting for us and cooking a lovely British dinner. I am so blessed to have such special friends. It only gets hard because there is such distance between our respective homes.

I had contacted James from the Munich airport and the only time he could see me was the next morning for breakfast, before he would be leaving for a few days holiday. George and Olivia reminded me of the way to the Wimbledon tube station and plotted out my stops to get to my meeting place with James. The next morning I was at the station by 7:00 a.m. I wouldn't be meeting James until 9:30 a.m. but wanted to allow extra time for getting lost.

On the tube, a woman sitting across from me was reading the local Metro newspaper, and on the front cover it read "Have you been abducted by aliens?" I laughed out loud because that's the only thing that really makes any sense in this nut-ball world. I got off the train at Oxford Circus. I was to meet James at a restaurant called Dishoom at 22 Kingly Street. I found my way there with plenty of time to spare so I walked the several blocks surrounding the restaurant taking in this magical city one more time. Talk about a radical extreme from the silence and peace of Bavaria. London is electric with energy, people, and sirens.

James arrived on his bike and was sporting bike shorts, helmet, and a zippy. We sat down at a small table, looked at each other, and in unison said "Wow, you look amazing!" My smile was back in full blossom and so was his. What a difference the past months had made for each of us. "Azul, you look amazing, so happy and healthy." I replied "*I am* so happy and healthy, and you James, you look like your happy self again." He was back in true form, jolly-green-giant laughter and all. We had been messaging during my journey, but now I had a chance to share in detail some of the most special moments and how those seeped life back into me at a cellular level. We belly laughed about the special massages with my Polish masseuse and how that experience woke up a resting sensuousness in me. I think an element of that well-laid look remained on my face, and my cheeks still ached from the laughter. James asked what I had learned and I replied, "I learned that I *can* make a great decision! This is the best and most important thing I have ever done for myself. I feel nourished at every level of my Being." He said "Yes Azul, I can see that. It is so nice to have you back."

"Well, right back at you James! Okay, spill it. You are in a totally different place than when I saw you in early June. Look at your smile, you're beaming! Did you have special massages too?" James cracked up and shared the details of his own reflective journey. He had a plan. He was going to leave London in February and embark on his own path of contemplating *Who Am I* and what he wants. The conversation was so gratifying, and our connection to one another had deepened even more now that we were both more fully present.

James had planned to leave after breakfast and go to work but he made a phone call and bought a couple of extra hours to spend together. We took a little stroll and went into some men's shops where James tried on jumpers. And then we popped into Hamleys Toy Shop where we ran amuck taking photos with giant gorillas, giraffes, Paddington Bear, and the Pillsbury Dough Boy. We even had an employee take photos of our ridiculousness for us. Talk about recapturing the youthfulness of childhood and spontaneous laughter. We were happy at a soul level and it poured out of us in every direction.

It was time for James to get to work so we walked back to Kingly Street where his bike was parked, and then he walked with me to Oxford Circus station. We hugged and hugged. It was terribly hard to say goodbye. If James and I lived in closer proximity, he is someone that I would enjoy spending time with. We have such a special connection. I would describe that connection as a communion with another soul. I am so grateful that my daughter brought him into our lives. He is one of the ones that I am sure I have shared other life experiences with. The connection runs much deeper than something that can blossom in just a single lifetime. James left on his bike and I walked down the stairs of the station. I made it down about two steps before the tears poured down my face. I didn't even try to stop them. I simply honored the feelings.

I changed trains at Nottinghill Gate and was back in Wimbledon in no time. George and Olivia were home waiting to hear about my day and to make our own plans for my remaining two days. George had been overwhelmed with a huge design project for the past several months and I could see the tiredness on his face. He was suggesting that we go hither and tither and do all of these grand things, but I suggested we stay local, go grab a bite to eat for dinner, and then spend the evening just catching up more on life. We drove to a local pub, enjoyed some bangers and mash, and then returned home and visited. George and I had met at the Chopra Center in 1995, and became fast and dear friends. I felt really blessed for the time I had to spend with them. Too much time had passed without seeing these precious people. My life at home lacks friendships with this level of deep connection. This is most certainly a crucial part of my deep desire to live and breathe a new story. It is not always easy though. I have never been one to just have a collection of friends. I am always looking for that soul connection, combined with a warped sense of humor and a deep sense of trust.

The next morning George logged on to his computer and shared photos of their long journey of building a home in Spain. George designed it and the home is just spectacular. He and Olivia shared stories of the slowness of the building process and the years it took to bring electricity to their home. Their stories were rich with experiences, new friends, favorite restaurants, and the peace that they both feel when they are there. Later that day we walked around the shops of Wimbledon. We enjoyed a simple day of smiles and togetherness. George had arranged for his daughter to join us the next day for an early afternoon meal. I requested that we go to their favorite local pub for fish and chips. Their son, Paul, would also be joining us.

I went to bed that night with disbelief that tomorrow would be the last day of my sojourn. It was so hard to get my head around how fast my journey had passed. I felt a million feelings as I drifted off to sleep. When I woke up the next morning my only wish was that the day would pass slowly so I could cherish every single second of it. My cases were packed and I did my double check for passport and alien card. I would need both to re-enter the USA. George knocked on my door and asked me to join him in his small upstairs office. He was printing out designs for me to take home for my children, and others were for me. He let me pick and choose my favorites. George is one of the most giving souls. With each visit we return home with some of his magical design creations. I have them hanging in my home and at every glance they bring a warm smile of the memories of this special friendship. George is an amazing graphic designer and has enjoyed a long, successful career which included designing album covers for a few legendary musicians. *Blessed friends.*

Around midday we all loaded into the car, made a quick stop to pick up Linda and then on to eat. We went to a pub called The Ship on the water's edge, ate fish and chips and enjoyed a pint. It was lovely. It had been a very long time since I had seen Linda, who was now all grown up and immersed in her professional career. Paul was delightful, and like all young people, finding his way in both a career and a home search. We lingered and I sucked it all in.

We arrived back at their home late afternoon and I asked for the phone number to arrange a ride to Heathrow the next morning. George was insisting that he drive me but I was insisting he did not. I had to leave by 5:00 a.m. to be at Heathrow two hours before my flight. I made arrangements for a driver. We said our goodbyes that night as I did not want to wake my gracious hosts so early in the morning.

At 4:50 a.m. on September 9, I walked out their front door and the driver was already there and waiting. He was a delightful man from Pakistan who shared stories of his life and of finding his way to the UK. About half way to the airport he said that we had plenty of time, and that if I would like, he'd find a place to stop and grab a "Spot of tea." I was in. He took the next exit and we drove to a petrol station where they knew him well. Thank goodness that even at petrol stations in London they know how to make a great cup of tea. I arrived at Heathrow two-and-a-half hours before my flight.

As I was in line to clear immigration, I reflected on the person who I was on June 7 when I was departing SeaTac, and all of the angst, exhaustion, and anguish that I carried with me that day. Now a whole new nourished, rested, revived, and strong woman occupied my mind, body, and spirit.

Again, I chuckled at what I might say to the Immigration Officer when he asked "What was the purpose of your trip?" I pondered saying "To wake-up, to remember who I really am, to deepen my awareness, and to run amuck." And in response to "What are you bringing back with you?" I *so* wanted to say, "This shit-eating grin on my face and hopefully no transmittable diseases." However, I simply stated that the purpose of my visit was to see dear friends and that I had nothing to declare. I learned a long time ago the hard way not to play with Immigration Officers. They don't find me funny at all.

After clearing immigration and security I wandered around for a bit, and then saw the same restaurant that I had sat and eaten breakfast in on June 13, after my first visit with James when I was heading to the Shakti Center in Schwabisch Hall, Germany. I entered the restaurant, sat in the same booth, ordered a cup of tea, opened up my laptop, and looked back through the thousands of photos I took on this sojourn. Every ounce of my Being filled with joy. Look what I had done! Look what I had experienced! I felt at home in my own essence again. *Best damn decision ever!* I was filled with love, light, and life in a way that I had forgotten was possible. My summer with no story had taught me how essential it is to live a new story. And I was ready.

Self-awareness is our most precious birthright.
We only have to choose to live by it.

Deepak Chopra

Chapter Nineteen

Homeward Bound

My flight was on time. I thanked God that I live in one of the most beautiful places in North America because I do not think I could have returned home if I didn't. I did, however, feel tremendous excitement to see my children and their partners, my family. I adore my family and I would be hugging them soon.

I boarded my flight, settled in, and wondered how challenging it would be to not step back into my same old story. I realized how thoughtful and conscientious I would have to be to live a new, healthier story. I also knew that as soon as I stepped off of the plane in Seattle, I would be right back in the midst of handling all of the estate business, looking for employment, and seeking my venue to share my message. I had decided while on this sojourn to take back possession of my home on the island, but was still undecided about whether I would list it for sale early next year or wait another year. I was crystal clear that I did not want to define my life around a burdensome mortgage. I had vowed to myself that I would no longer knock on doors of those who will not hear, as my way of finding a venue to share my message. I had made a commitment to myself that I would return home and find a way to have a simple, stress-free, and fulfilled life. Seattle is known for its horrible traffic congestion. I was not willing to spend any more of the precious moments of my life sitting in traffic. I inhaled a very long, deep breath and prayed to never forget how I felt in that moment and to never forget the devotion I felt to live a new story. I was also fully aware of how others would work diligently to make sure that I continued to live the same old story, and insist that I remain a participant in aspects of their stories. I suspected my non-participation could produce quite a rippling affect.

It was a nine-and-a-half-hour flight, arriving in Seattle at noon on the same day. I took out my notepad and started to flesh out more of what calls me to death and dying. I reflected on the death of my own life story and the excitement of telling and living a new story. I held an uncompromising intention to live a much more nurturing story, a loving story, an easier story, and a story with so much less drama. I knew the only way to accomplish that was with awareness and with the blind refusal to fall back into the trap of others who are more comfortable with my old story. I just could not do it. I wondered which friendships may fall by the wayside and which new friendships might grace my life. I did know that I wanted to surround myself with kind, light, healthy, fun-loving, and consciously evolving people. I am also aware that we attract into our lives who we are at any given moment. So *Who Am I* now? In this moment I am lightness, I am love, I am joy, I am healed, whole, and holy with a message in my heart that may one day serve to touch another's life. Deepak's words "Healing is a holy act" flashed through my mind. And I smiled.

I spent the entire flight reflecting on the ego deaths in my life and how I perceive these ego deaths to be full of potentiality to help us discover *who and why we really are.* I believe that for every one of us, each ego death *gifts* us the opportunity to be transformed. Ego deaths to me mean the death of identifying so strongly with I am this and I am that, and our unending focus on the physicality of life. We all play numerous roles throughout our lives. Playing these roles is simply part of our human experience but identifying strongly with these roles is the business of the ego. It is only the ego that is terrified of dying.

I again reflected on the ego deaths in my own life, starting with the divorce of my parents when I was four years old. What died? What died was my relationship with my father as I knew it. What died was my experience as a child having a mom and dad and family all together. Now what was extraordinary, and probably because I was so young, I had started to hone my natural ability to connect with Spirit through my childlike way of meditating by visually stripping away everything in my environment, until all I experienced was safety and peace. I used to sit on the floor in my bedroom up against a wall with my eyes closed, and I would mentally strip away the furnishings in the room, and then strip away the rest of the suite we lived in. Next, I would strip away the whole house, the yard, the park across the street, and then all of the sudden I was enveloped in peace and a feeling of comfort and safety. Today, I would describe that feeling as an experience of being held in the womb of creation. I do believe that we are all born with these natural abilities. And I also think that by about age six or seven, we are so immersed in the hypnosis of social conditioning that we lose sight of these natural states and of the essence of *Who We Really Are*. But it was the grace of this ego death that pulled me closer to Spirit. It wasn't until 1995, when I was formally instructed in Primordial Sound Meditation, had embraced the practice in my life, and had begun to access pure consciousness, that I remembered those experiences that I had as a four-year-old through my childlike way of meditating.

I reflected on my eleven-year journey as a student pursuing my degrees, and the unanticipated absolute sense of feeling lost that I experienced when I finally completed my master's degree. I was truly excited to be finished with that arduous path. I felt blessed to have learned all that I had learned. But I also felt this unusual sense of loss. I was no longer a graduate student. I was no longer student number 8424490. Who was I now? The education path took up such a huge part of my life and it was a huge part of my story. Now what? I ached for campus and for professors and mentors. It was another ego death, another death of the story that I had been living, and another opportunity to discover *Who and Why I Really Am*. It was 1992, and I was seeking.

Shortly after graduating, I woke up one morning with the idea to volunteer one day a week at Seattle Children's Hospital, and they quickly trained me for the hematology/oncology unit. There they were, my new little, bald-headed teachers. And that experience became the out loud impetus that called me to engage in dialogues about death and dying. I vividly remember the day I was holding a six-week-old baby in my arms. She had cancer. I held her and asked her "What is your purpose little one? Why have you come for what seems like such a short amount of time? What can you teach us?" At that moment her young teenage mom came into the room and started to share how her boyfriend never wanted the baby and how he would beat her during her pregnancy. She said that she did not want the baby either. In that instant things made sense to me. I understood how an infant, even in the womb, could metabolize that experience. It was, to me, a cancerous situation. I also understood that that small baby's presence held within it the possibility to teach these two young people the ability to love unconditionally. She was a little tiny messenger who made a brave choice to show up briefly to teach a lesson of love.

During those five-years of Mondays I spent a great deal of time with the children, many of whom died. They taught me so much, especially to not fear death. The younger they were, the less fear they appeared to experience. I truly believe that their memories of *Who They Really Are* were fresh. Ego has not taken its hold on them as it does as we grow older. They all brought with them the possibility for parents, siblings, and the medical professionals serving them, to know unconditional love. These children were the most special messengers that I had ever encountered. My heart ached for their parents. To lose a child is the kind of experience that most of us never get over. I dearly loved my own children and I quickly embraced them even more fully. I wanted desperately to provide a context for parents and medical professionals to be able to engage in conversations about death and dying.

That's when the knocking on doors started. I used to think "Yeah but who is really going to listen to a thirty-four-year-old talk about death and dying." What credibility did I have? That is one of the greatest things about being fifty-nine years old, I now have more life under my belt and more credibility. Lord knows that many people in our North American culture, especially employers, perceive me as someone who could drop dead at any moment. How did this experience offer me an opportunity for another ego death? The experience gifted me the opportunity to really start to question *Who Am I* separate from this physical body? Their presence in my life also exposed *Why Am I* by igniting my passion to openly discuss death and dying, and to discover the healing gift those conversations bring. The blessing was that I got to observe the fearless, innocent, and graceful way that these children encountered death. And with them, I was blessed with the opportunity to engage in the most innocent and delicious dialogues that I had ever experienced. These young mentor messengers wanted to talk about death. They asked questions like "Do you think that Jesus knew he was going to die? Do you know when you are going to die, like I do?" They wanted to give their toys to their siblings before they died. They wanted to tell "Mommy and daddy that when I leave I am going to be fine and not to feel so sad." They wanted to talk about death and dying.

Throughout my flight home, I continued to reflect on all of the deaths of roles I have played and the attachment that I have had to those roles. There were so many of them. I remembered when my children were both grown and had left home on their own adventures, how I had wandered around the grocery store for well over an hour trying to figure out what I liked to eat and what movie I wanted to rent. I had been "Mom" for so long, focused on their likes and their interests, that I didn't have a clue what I liked. We do that as moms. I ran my ticker tape of my lifetime of experiences as mom. It was really front and center for me even as I began this sojourn. I realized when I was at the Shakti Center at the beginning of this journey, that even with Jet's death I had been focused on my children and their loss of their father. I hadn't even begun to process that loss for myself. I hadn't even begun to feel the depth of the loss of Jet's presence in my own life and in my heart. I hadn't even realized the state of shock that I had been experiencing. We had played the roles of each other's friend, lover, spouse, co-parent, and variations of those roles for thirty-six years. We had also played the roles of boss and employee. My heart felt this huge hole. My life felt a huge hole. It was another whirlwind of opportunities to discover *Who Am I*?

So what is death? What dies? My response to those questions today is that we are not this body and we are not this brain. We are something much more profound. As Wayne Dyer often said "We are not human beings having occasional spiritual experiences, we are spiritual beings having occasional human experiences." I believe that we are part of a higher stream of consciousness. We come from consciousness, we exist in consciousness, and we relocate in consciousness. So what dies? The skin-encapsulated Ego dies. The physical body dies? But *who we really are* does not die. We relocate. We simply resonate to higher frequencies.

How do I know this? Why do I believe this? I *know* it because it resonates with my lived experience. And because I have metabolized a level of awareness, a higher state of consciousness, which allows me to see and experience connections with the ones I love who have transitioned. I am sure that it also resonates with many of your own experiences. However, we often just carry these experiences silently within because we haven't yet had the curiously open context to discuss them freely, or we have been too afraid of how we might be judged if we do share.

Let me break tradition and share some of mine. Throughout my life, from the time I was a teenager, I have continued to experience relationships with the people I have loved dearly, and who died and transitioned to another frequency. When Angelica, my mom's friend who had been such a special presence in my life, died; I took a long walk in the park across the street and I felt her with me. The sky was the most unusual crimson color and I heard her laughter. She said that she felt well for the first time in a long time. I heard her voice. She has also visited me in my dreams when I have been going through difficult times. She just appears with a loving smile on her face. And when my best friend and first love died, at his funeral which was an open-coffin funeral, I touched his face and his hands and I knew that we are not this body. I *knew* it! I felt him all around me. On my flight home that evening I felt his freedom and his happiness so fully that I cried tears of sheer happiness with him. It was one of the most profound moments of joy that I have ever experienced.

When my lifelong friend, Denzel, was dying I went to visit him and we spent a day pondering death. We went to the church where his service would be held, and then we walked out to the spot where he would be buried to look at his view. We lingered for an hour or so and talked about how he should be positioned in the ground to optimize his view, and we laughed. We also visited his father's grave and talked all day about our thoughts on death. He shared that he definitely did not want to be cremated because it terrified him that the ashes given to his family may not be his ashes. I shared with him that I'd never had a thought like that about cremation and that I didn't care if the ashes given to my loved ones were my ashes, but that I definitely did not want to be rotting in a grave eaten by worms and maggots. We shared a great belly laugh over our concerns. Later that afternoon, we listened to a CD which I had brought with me called *Being a Compassionate Companion* from the Zen Hospice Project, and on it a story called the *Mustard Seed* was told. It really resonated with both of us. A month later on the drive to Denzel's funeral there was a sign next to the road that read "The Mustard Seed." There was no apparent reason for that sign to be placed where it was. Further along the drive "Denzel" was written on the road, on the pavement itself. Nobody saw it except Denzel's wife and children, and my daughter and me.

When my father was dying I did not make it in time to see him. He was diagnosed with cancer and died so quickly. When we spoke on the phone, shortly after his diagnosis, I told him I would come in a couple of weeks as soon as my quarter was over and my grading was completed. He died the week before I got there. A few weeks later I drove up to Penticton, BC from Seattle. My sister took my children and me to my father's apartment where we spent the night. Lying on my father's bed was the shirt he had last worn with his blood still on it behind the collar. He had had a cancerous tumor on the back of his neck that was strangulating his spine. Late at night I sat on the edge of his bed, hugged that shirt, and told my father how sorry I was that I didn't make it in time to see him. Right at that moment I felt my father sit next to me on the bed and put his arm around me, and he told me that I could say goodbye now. Then he kissed my right cheek and I held and kissed his left arm which was draped over my left shoulder. It was one of the most precious moments of my entire life. I literally felt his peace and his joy. Nobody, absolutely nobody, can convince me that those were not real experiences. They were as real as any moment I have experienced with the living.

My sister has met me in my dreams and given me consistent little nudges when I have been pondering life changes and directions to head. She emphatically told me in a dream one night not to be involved in a relationship with the galloping man. I should have listened. Wayne Dyer has come to me in several dreams, and on one of his visits we were in a car together and he was driving fast on a beautiful, windy, country road and he said to me "Isn't this fun and free, just enjoy the journey of it all. And don't worry, I couldn't possibly be better." My dear friend Ben, who I nicknamed "Hawk Feather," has dropped many hawk feathers on my path, even on city blocks or in shopping malls where you'd never expect to see them and I have interpreted those as signposts that he's right here and walking beside me.

When Jet died and my children and I were packing up his home, I heard him say "Look inside." I slept in his bed that night and one of the side table lights started to flicker. I asked Jet if it was him and the light flickered again. I told him that I had heard his words to "Look inside," and that I was fairly certain that he didn't mean to look inside myself because he never spoke of that type of introspection. I started to ask a series of questions about the location in his home where I was to look inside. I started with "Is it in the kitchen, or the living room, or the family room, or the memory room?" There was no flicker of the light and then it occurred to me that I had asked the series of questions in rapid order. So I started again and asked "Is it in the kitchen?" No flicker. "Is it in the living room?" No flicker. When I got to "Is it in the memory room?" The light flickered. I told him that I got the message and that the next day I would be packing the contents of the memory room and I would diligently look inside everything. I suspected that I was looking for a manila envelope with cash in it because it was a thing that Jet did. He would save ten, twenty, and fifty dollar bills, in increments of one hundred dollars, with post-it notes on them indicating the dates he put them in the envelope. The next day while I was packing the memory room, which was a little back room in his home with dozens of framed photos of our life and which he used as a back office, I heard him say again "Look inside." I can't begin to tell you how large a volume of paperwork was in the office, the desk, the cupboards, and the closets. He repeated "Look inside." I caught myself arguing out loud with him at one point stating that I was in fact looking inside everything. Then I found an accordion folder that contained several files labeled life insurance. I knew I would need to go through that folder thoroughly. He had known, in my role as Executor, that I would do that. I sat with that accordion folder and looked through every manila file and every piece of paper. It contained dated and expired policies and personal information. I set the accordion folder aside and was proceeding to the next drawer when I heard him *shout* at me "Look inside." I assured him that I had looked inside every single manila file in that accordion folder, but again he said "Look inside." So I entertained him and took each of the manila files out of the accordion folder, and underneath those files was a scrunched up manila envelope. I opened it and there was five-thousand dollars, in one-hundred-dollar-increments, with post-its paper clipped to them. I laughed out loud and then cried. I looked up and said "Got it." I never heard him say "Look inside" after that.

When my daughter has been going through difficult times of transition in her life, her father has shown me in my dreams that he is carrying her. He has literally been holding her in his arms, walking with her, or carrying her piggyback style. Our daughter typically appears as a small child in these dreams and her father, the strong protector. There have been many of those dreams. One night, while carrying our daughter, her father handed me a small yellow flower and said that everything was going to be just fine. When I woke in the morning there was a small yellow flower lying on the top of my comforter near the bottom of my bed. My horse, Topanas, has played a similar role for me. Through my most difficult times of transition, he has shown up and I am riding him, running as fast as he could run and carrying me through.

There was a night about two years ago that I was lying in bed and feeling so lost in my life. I was talking with God et al. and asking and begging for my grief and pain to pass. I was asking from the depths of my Being for help in finding comfort. I was in a state of such emotional agony. I was laying on my right side and just rocking myself to find comfort, and all of a sudden a Being laid down next to me, spooned with me, and enveloped me in the most loving comfort I have ever known. I laid there silent just thinking *thank you, thank you, thank you!* As I felt relief, the Being left. I don't know who it was that held that space for me that night but it was a true turning point in healing my grief.

I have had dozens of these experiences with transitioned souls. I only wish I would have journaled and documented them as they happened. I am sure many, if not most of you, have had similar experiences and hold them dear to your heart. I would love to hear from you if you are willing to share. Please write them down and send them to me. I will also gladly share my stories and welcome you sharing your stories at my speaking engagements and events. I believe it is essential for our conscious evolution that these stories be shared. Let's give them voice and in doing so, discover *Who We Really Are.*

So when we die, what dies? Who dies? The physical body dies. The brain dies. The Ego dies. But *Who We Really Are* does not die. We are pure consciousness. *Who We Really Are*, consciousness, uses our brains as transmitters and our bodies as vessels to manifest human experiences. Why? For our own conscious evolution, that's why. *Who We Really Are* is omnipotent, omniscient, and holy. Discovering *Who We Really Are* is the only path to knowing *Why We Are* and to leading fulfilled, purposeful lives by utilizing our unique gifts and talents in the service of others.

Your mind, this globe of awareness, is a starry
universe. When you push off with your foot, a
thousand new roads become clear.

Rumi

Chapter Twenty

A Call to Consciousness

The pilot had just announced that we were about ninety minutes away from our destination and that the temperature in Seattle was seventy degrees and sunny. My stomach flipped a bit and I inhaled a long, deep breath, and wondered what lay ahead of me as I stepped off of the plane. I felt overwhelmed with a mixture of both sadness that my sojourn had come to an end, and elation to get to see the people I love so much. I acknowledged to myself that my *awarefulness* journey will never end. I can be aware and work to continuously expand my awareness wherever I am. I also felt grateful to have traveled enough in my life, each time returning with tons of photographs and stories to share, and had learned that even my best friends didn't really want to hear all of the stories. I discovered that it is a rare bird indeed that wants to sit and look at photographs. That has always been a bit of a mystery to me. I am just the opposite. I can't wait to hear the stories of others' adventures and I can spend hours looking at their pictures. I wonder why people don't engage more that way. I personally think they are missing out.

As we got nearer to Seattle, I remembered an email that I had received during my last days in London from an author and coach who I deeply admire. Her name is Tama Kieves and her email was announcing that she would be giving a talk in Seattle on September 13. It continued to say that she would also be available for one-on-one coaching sessions. I couldn't believe the timing but I also disregarded the possibility of meeting with her for a coaching session because I was at the tail end of my budget. I had spent it well and loved every single moment of it. Tama's first book, *This Time I Dance*, was released in 2002. I bought a copy when it was released, read it, and then purchased a couple of copies for other people who I thought might enjoy her work. Over the ensuing years I re-read that book, purchased and read her next books, *A Year without Fear* and *Inspired and Unstoppable*. She is one of the most uplifting female spiritual Beings to have crossed my path.

We touched down on the runway at SeaTac and the tears started to pour down my cheeks. I felt like I would love to hug my kids, enjoy a weekend together, and then get back on the plane. I took several deep breaths and exited the aircraft. My children both live at a distance and I knew that nobody would be greeting me at the airport. It was a Friday, noontime, and a work day for everyone. Plus, I really wanted to have a moment in time to regroup and adjust to being back. I would not be able to take back possession of my home for two days so I stayed in a hotel in downtown Seattle. I was back home in the Pacific Northwest, but more than anything I was at home within myself. I spent a quiet evening. The next morning I caught the ferry from downtown Seattle to the island and spent the night at Adara's home. My body clock was totally off and I was starting to feel the jet lag. We had a nice evening and reflected on our time in Amsterdam and Prague. The next morning I went to my home. I had left most of my furnishings in my home when I leased it. It was so strange walking back into my life, *almost eerie.* My home wasn't in the condition that I would have maintained it but it was fixable. The energy in it definitely felt different but nothing that a good *saging* wouldn't clear. Somewhere, in those first two days after my return, I received another email reminder that Tama would be speaking in Seattle on September 13, and that she still had time available in her schedule for a one-on-one session. I said to myself "Oh screw money," and I signed up for a session. Two days later I hopped back on the ferry. My time with Tama was scheduled for an hour, a couple of hours before she was to speak. I was so incredibly excited to meet her in person. I had also just a hit a major jet lag wall but nothing was going to stop me from seeing her.

She was speaking at the Unity Church in Seattle. I arrived early and was wandering around inside when I heard someone knocking loudly on the front door. As I approached the door I could see it was Tama. I think my heart actually skipped a beat with excitement. I opened the door and introduced myself. We quickly decided that since it was such a gorgeous day, we would sit outside on a little private patio and talk. I apologized for my jet-lagged induced exhaustion and then began to share how I had just spent my last ninety-two days. I told her of my struggle to find a venue for my heart's work, and that I have ached to write for years but never knew exactly how to focus my writing, or how to share the calling that I felt so deeply in my Being. She was as genuine and as enthusiastic in person as she is in her writing. She is alive with this amazing electric energy and *Oh my God* her laughter is infectious. It was a truly enjoyable hour. Nearing the end of our time together she looked at me and said "Well, it seems to me that you have figured it out." I asked "Figured out what?" She replied "Your venue, a book. And what you are to write about, write about your ninety-two days." As those words left her lips my whole Being lit up. *Of course it was!* In that moment I felt the absolute rightness of what Tama had just suggested. A smile blossomed in me from my baby toes to the tip of my head. I gave her a huge hug, thanked her profusely, and left to catch the ferry. I wanted to stay and listen to her talk that evening but I had hit a wall of overwhelming tiredness.

The next morning I was moving my boxes of personal belongings out of storage and back into my home. I spent the weekend unpacking and making my home a home again. When all of my precious belongings were in place, I sat on my couch late in the evening and took it all in. I looked at my antiquarian books, some of which are two hundred years old, and many of my other treasures from various European trips. I looked around at my favorite possessions: my grandfather clock, my framed black-and-white photographs nicely hung on my walls, and my one-hundred-and-fifty-year-old dining room table. And then I experienced the most unanticipated bizarre feeling. I sat there and thought "Can I even relate to these possessions anymore? Are these things confining me to something I no longer am?" I have loved these treasures so it was the most *astonishing* feeling!

Over the next days and weeks I had the opportunity to see my dear loved ones, which was just extraordinary. I was also reimmersed in the estate business full time and all the while I was crucially aware of my desire to live a new story. The world of estate professionals continued to view me and mine in the same fashion as they did before my sojourn. Their opinions hadn't changed *but I had*. I now felt free of their opinions of me. I had a lot of things to put in order so I could stay the course, and I was committed to making the time to honor myself and to write.

The first many weeks home were also really tough ones with reference to reassembling my life. I felt pressure to figure out how to sustain my mortgage and home expenses, to return to the status of being gainfully employed, and to hold tight to living a healthier story. There were certainly moments when I felt a great deal of sadness and I ached to be back in Europe. My friends were happy to see me and I them. But some of their stories were shockingly loud with things and ways of being that I could just no longer be a part of. A few expressed an interest in my travels, but an interest of never longer than an hour. I carried my laptop with me to share photos of my journey. There was only one person who spent time looking at them and who was fully present to hear of my adventure, my daughter.

Over the next month or so I was astonished by how loud the cultural hypnosis was to me. The hypnosis that we typically exist in without questioning its power and validity, and which serves as a determining factor in shaping our core beliefs. I felt like my sojourn had produced a mega dose of clarity that was all around me and everywhere. Before my ninety-two days of self-reflection, I had over the decades, metabolized a level of awareness that at times made it more challenging to maneuver among people who accepted the cultural hypnosis without question. Now I was feeling even more like a foreigner in my homeland. I also had a heightened awareness of low energy environments and was learning to spend as little time as possible in those contexts. I didn't feel dislike for the people in those environments. Instead, I felt like surrounding them with love and then leaving as quickly as possible. I am aware every single day and with every single encounter I have with people, that I can choose which components to take with me, to rise above, to walk away from, and which components that I want to give life to in my story.

I have often felt that the United States is one of the more unhealthy countries, of the developed countries in the world, and now it feels even more so. Please don't misunderstand, I think it is a great country in many ways and affords freedoms and lifestyle choices which millions in our world population will never know. And I feel blessed to live here. We have access to superior education, healthcare (if we can afford it), and extremely comfortable lifestyles. I also see the consciousness as dominated by consumerism, materialism, reality television shows, and led by a narcissistic sociopathic President; who, shockingly to me, maintains a level of popularity with way too large a percentage of our population. That said, I think that I can now see the gift of Donald Trump's election to the highest and most respected office in our country. It is a call, a *scream* if you will, for each of us to embrace our own shadow. As I mentioned in the beginning of this book, he represents a darkness that has the possibility to exist within each of us. His darkness is out loud and extreme. He is exposing the political darkness of the country and of the citizens of this country who continue to admire and support him;

and the darkness of those of us who do not support him but are enraged by him. It's all darkness. He is also part of the same larger consciousness that each of us is a part of.

Media describes him as a warring, mean, intolerant, defiant, bigoted, selfish, egotistical, and arrogant human being. I hear you, those words sound so *judgy, judgy, judgy*. But don't get your panties in a bunch, they are not my words. They are the common words often used to describe this leader, though I will say that I don't disagree with them. I ask you to feel the frequencies of those descriptive words and of the associated behaviors. Say them. Feel them. Now compare those feelings to the feelings you experience with the frequencies of these descriptive words and associated behaviors: integrity, compassion, humility, acceptance, cooperation, creativity, intelligence, grace, and vision. Do you feel the difference? Trump's choices keep him locked in the lowest frequencies of consciousness. Or better yet, a state of unconsciousness. Unbeknownst to him, his role as President of the United States is a call to each of us to become fully aware and we cannot do that without embracing and examining our own shadow selves.

We have been summoned. It is time for each of us to embark on a journey to *awarefulness*. To discover *Who You Are* and *Why You Are*, and you just can't get there without examining your shadow self, your thoughts, and the consciousness that has shaped and formed your story. We have to get beyond our stories, beyond our egos, and make way for our unique contributions to a higher consciousness. We cannot transition an Ego to a higher state. We cannot meet darkness with darkness. We can however, become aware and awake in our *awarefulness*. We can exude light.

We can change the consciousness one person at a time and it is our responsibility to do so. Take the leap. Examine your story. Look and look deeply within. I promise you that if you are willing to see the shadows that exist within you and take responsibility for your thoughts and behaviors, there is exquisite health, freedom, peace, and joy just waiting for you to seize it. I am a believer that the *Universe* conspires on our behalf, constantly nudging us in the direction of conscious evolution. I often think about the conspiracy that made this journey to *awarefulness* possible for me. If Jet wouldn't have gotten sick, if I wouldn't have leased out my home, if Jet wouldn't have died, if my children hadn't received a bit of money from their father, if my daughter hadn't gifted some of it to me, if the management team where I was employed would have followed through on their promise to vet my education programs, if the homeowner's association hadn't required me to lease out my home for a minimum of a year, if I hadn't reached a place of feeling broken, then this brilliant opportunity to discover *Who I Am* and *Why I Am* would not likely have happened; at least not when it did. I wouldn't have considered it a possibility at this time. But it was a possibility and it is for you too.

How do you get started? *Turn off the damn news!* I turned off the news in 1995. Some people criticize me for that and have even suggested that I am ignorant because I refuse to start and finish each day listening to the horror and drama of the world. I disagree. I stay informed. It is very hard not to with all of the technology bombarding us with news at every possible moment. I suggest that you allow yourself thirty minutes each day to select which headlines you would like to read or listen to, followed by an hour of reading or listening to the good news happening in the world. And meditate, every day, meditate. The world needs more of our feminine energy and it needs us to be nourished, healed, and self-aware. With each healing and each awakened *awarefulness*, we heal humanity.

I *am* at home within myself in ways that are so delicious. *Who Am I?* I am consciousness. I am love. I am pure joy. I am soulful. I am awareness. I am light. *I simply am.* What is next? Consciously living a healthier story! Living the *Why I Am* and sharing a message placed so deeply in my soul that may serve to help others on their own journeys to *awarefulness*.

Printed in the United States
By Bookmasters